The World War That Changed the Story of Women

Maximilian Natal

NATAL PUBLISHING LLC
ARS LONGA, VITA BREVIS

CONTENTS

Chapter One

"The First World War was the great military and political event of its time; but it was also the great imaginative event. It altered the ways in which men and women thought not only about war but about the world."   —*Samuel Hynes*

English philosopher Herbert Spencer said that nothing was more disruptive to a society's institutions than war. Once a country reorganized its social structures and economy around military conflict, there was very little chance of going back to the way things were before the hostilities.

World War One provides a perfect example of this axiom. In many ways, 1914 (the first year of the war) was the hinge upon which the rest of modern history turned. For instance, with the relative newness of mass media, the war inaugurated a novel concept called "propaganda". A tool of psychological warfare, it was initially assumed that it would end after the war, but didn't. An additional change that remains with us today is the use of passports to travel between countries (first issued in 1915). Furthermore, Daylight Savings Time was inaugurated in England in 1916 (and in the United States in 1918) as a method by which to get more labor out of workers to aid the war effort. Another innovation that occurred was the expansion of social welfare programs (brought about by the introduction of veteran's benefits). Yet another paradigm shift was the normalization of women in the workplace.

The latter circumstance arose because of the massive numbers of war dead, whereupon women were called upon to fill those jobs in the factories vacated by millions of male fatalities. Mass death has always been a catalyst for social change, and, ironically, the expansion of rights. After the Black Plague in the 1300s, for instance, one-third of Europe lay dead. The sudden labor shortage panicked the aristocracy, whose wealth was tied up in the land. To coax surviving workers back into the fields, they had to come up with attractive inducements for the peasants. One of these was increased political rights and the end of serfdom.

World War One was, in many ways, a synthetic version of this phenomenon. With the number of casualties brought about by the Great War (as it was then known), an expansion of suffrage and political rights ensued.

English historian Alistair Horne, in holding forth about World War One, said, "To the women of France the war had brought an emancipatory revolution. Never had they been so great a power in the country. At the outbreak of war, to a woman, they had rushed off to become nurses, filled the administrative gaps left by men, worked in the munitions factories. The soldiers grumbled on returning home to find their wives turned yellow by picric acid. But they had little redress."

It bears pointing out in a digression that, though the picric acid used in shells tended to turn a person's skin yellow, their spouse's concerns may not have been purely aesthetic. In "The First World War: A Complete History," by Martin Gilbert, he says, "The dangers were ever-present. Women working with the explosive TNT were jocularly referred to as 'canaries' because of the yellow discoloration of the skin which was a symptom of TNT poisoning. Sixty-one women munitions workers died of poisoning, and eighty-one in other accidents at work. In accidental explosions during the war, seventy-one women were killed, one at the factory at Gretna, sixty-nine at Silvertown in East London, when seventy-two women were also severely injured."

Danger aside, British historian John Ramsden commented, "Increasingly [women] had greater independence. They were more likely to be earning good money. They were more likely to be earning from their own work and not simply through something related to their husband or their father. They had some freedom—sometimes because they'd moved away from the family home to go and live in a place nearer to a factory. They could live a more independent social life. They were more likely to smoke and they were more likely to be wearing cosmetics. These are all statements of independence."

Of course, all rapid and disruptive social change is apt to cause trepidation—especially in people whose broader frame-of-reference gives them some notion of how things were before. In "Women and the First World War," by Susan Grayzel, she bodies forth some of the anxieties expressed at the time. She writes, "By the end of 1916, articles in Britain's *Daily Express* were asking if 'War Times Loosen Manners and Morals?', referring specifically to the use of 'strong language' by women, while the following year Max Pemberton was addressing the question 'Are Women Losing Men's Respect?' in *Pearson's Weekly* (*Daily Express*, 5 December 1916; *Pearson's Weekly*, 29 September 1917). In these and other accounts by journalists, a palpable transformation had occurred in women's manners, their use of vulgarity, appearance in shorter skirts or male attire or make up, and their adoption of habits like smoking."

Of course, even before the war, some keen prognosticators, like H.G. Wells, had an inkling of social changes to come. In his 1900 book "Anticipations," Wells hazarded some predictions about the next hundred years. He correctly saw women with short hair and pants as he noted that gender differentiation in clothing would diminish. He wrote, "It is an interesting thing to speculate how far the characteristic difference in the dress of men and women is likely to be modified by the changes in the mechanical fabric of the social order. In the past, when men have toiled at the plough, or with the harrow, or in the hunting-field, and women have sat still at home, or been at the most domestic drudges, it was inevitable that their clothing should become profoundly differentiated. But now that men and women are coming to resemble each other more and more in their way of life, both are becoming sedentary, both are becoming active; both at last are emerging side by side from the sweat-shop of toil into the open spaces of an intellectually and physically active life, where exercise, sometimes gentle, sometimes hard, is part of the daily rule; it follows that their clothing will assimilate, and be adapted in a like manner to the same uses."

This standardization, so characteristic of the Industrial Age (where philosophers like Gabriel Marcel worried about the appearance of what he called "Mass Man") represent something of a reversal from historical norms, which usually favored differentiation.

The Division of Labor

In "The Study of Sociology," the aforementioned Herbert Spencer discussed how, in primitive societies, there was more democracy and less hierarchical structure. People, he said, weren't differentiated by segregation of duties. That is to say, every caveman was expected to have the same skills and make his own shelter, find his own food, engage in his own healthcare, and so forth. Each individual was expected to be a self-contained unit. Only as society gets more complex do we see a division of labor. Herbert Spencer equates this phenomenon with stem cells in the infancy of an organism. But, as the creature gets more complex, the generic stem cells differentiate into heart cells, brain cells, arm cells, etc. To quote Spencer as he applies this to the evolution of societies: "These differences of function, and consequent differences of structure, at first feebly marked, slight in degree, and few in kind, become, as organization progresses, definite and numerous; and in proportion as they do this the requirements are better met. Now structural traits expressible in the same language, distinguish lower and higher types of societies from one another; and distinguish the earlier stages of each society from the later. Primitive tribes show no established contrasts of parts. At first all men carry on the same kinds of activities, with no dependence on one another, or but occasional dependence. There is not even a settled chieftainship; and only in times of war is there a spontaneous and temporary subordination to those who show themselves the best leaders. From the small unformed social aggregates thus characterized, the progress is towards social aggregates of increased size, the parts of which acquire unlikenesses that become ever greater, more definite, and more multitudinous. The units of the society as it evolves, fall into different orders of activities, determined by differences in their local conditions or their individual powers; and there slowly result permanent social structures, of which the primary ones become decided while they are being complicated by secondary ones, growing in their turns decided, and so on."

In his foundational economics classic "The Wealth of Nations," Adam Smith ponders why some societies grow rich, while others stagnate and remain poor. His answer to this question was what he famously called "the division of labor". He wrote, "The greatest improvements in the productive powers of labour, and the greater part of the skill, dexterity, and judgment, with which it is anywhere directed, or applied, seem to have been the effects of the division of labour. The effects of the division of labour, in the general business of society, will be more easily understood, by considering in what manner it operates in some particular manufactures."

He then gives his famous example of a pin factory. A single worker, doing all the steps himself, might turn out ten pins a day. However, if you break up the six or seven steps to make a pin, and assign different workers to each of those steps, the line-workers gain in competence and speed due to their familiarity with their particular step—with the result being that output goes from 10 pins a day to 10,000 pins.

To believe anthropologists, the same factors were in play when society engaged in a division of labor along gender lines. Thus, in the 20th Century, scholars began speaking in terms of "Hunter-gatherer societies," in which men stalked big game, while women (tied to children) remained back at camp, and foraged for roots and berries. It's likely that women became our first artists and doctors as they discovered plants for pigments and medicines.

Ernestine Friedl, in her 1975 book "Women and Men: An Anthropologist's View," explicitly discussed the gendered division of labor in hunter-gatherer societies, analyzing how men's hunting and women's gathering roles were not only practical but also influenced social status and power dynamics. Anthropologists Julian Steward, Lewis Binford, Richard B. Lee and Irven DeVore have all contributed to the literature of hunter-gatherer societies and explained its general benefits to the respective civilizations they studied.

When the Change Came

The Industrial Revolution, which initially inspired Adam Smith to document this phenomenon in more advanced, market-based societies ironically saw a reversal of this trend.

Before the Industrial Revolution, families tended to live on self-contained farms. Mother, father, children, aunts, uncles, cousins and grandparents all coexisted on a single property, each assigned their special jobs. Father might till the soil, while his sons would sow the seeds and bring in the harvest. Meanwhile, Mother might spin the loom and make textiles to clothe everyone, as an uncle might be the blacksmith for the plantation, with an aunt churning butter or tending to chickens. Even grandparents served a purpose, babysitting young children or dispensing wisdom to succeeding generations.

The family, at this historical period, ran like a corporation, with the father at the top as *paterfamilias*. He was a sort of CEO, who not only saw to the economic interests of the farm-compound, but also arranged marriages for his children. These marriages were less about love-alliances than about finding suitable spouses with shared values and interlocking economic interests. It was less emotion-based than logic-based, with hormones playing far less a role in wedlock and *mésalliances* being rarer.

Interestingly, author Eric Barker provides some shocking stats about how arranged marriages have far higher success rates than modern romantic notions of matrimony (which wear off at around time that the hormones do). Studies, for instance, have shown that divorce rates for couples where an impartial match-maker brokers the marriage were less than 4%, as opposed to random, emotion-based marriages that have a 56% failure rate.

People like Douglas Gairdner see a clear role for parents in the selection of mates for their children and bemoaned the side-effects of the Industrial Revolution, which saw the transition from the extended family to the much-smaller "nuclear family" (composed only of parents and two children). In his book "The War Against the Family," he writes, "With industrialization, however, and then with 18th century Enlightenment ideas, there came a transition and a change in mentality. People flocked to cities. Money became common as a means of exchange, and with it the idea of profits and the growth of a labouring class to supply them. The ordinary household changed radically as production increasingly took place in factories instead of the home. Private property became all important. So the household shrank in numbers, closed its doors to the community, and became a limited private space, mirroring the private property basis of capitalism. Social life became increasingly contractual, and children began to assume more rights against parents and exert more choice over marriage and future. In short, individuals were no longer subordinated to community. What Stone calls 'Affective Individualism' began to replace both kinship and community. The family became a mirror of the capitalist society it nurtured, for which it turned out little producers."

Economic historians tell us that the Industrial Revolution had profound consequences for the larger society. As factories rose up, they required workers. To seduce young men away from family farms, they initially offered them handsome wages if they left their hamlet and moved to the city. The effect on the old feudal farm-structure was catastrophic as fathers could no longer rely on sons to help them sow the fields. As youths left the provinces for urban areas, farms collapsed (resulting in the decline of food surpluses and famine). It got so bad, according to Thomas Malthus, that it eventually would cost a worker a week's wages to buy a loaf of bread.

So as industrialization led to the mass production of commercial goods like shoes, or playing cards, or textiles, it ironically conduced to the rise in the scarcity of necessities like food.

The collapse of the old feudal family-structure also saw the diminishment of the relevance of the father, who no longer occupied the role of *paterfamilias*.

But it had other wide-ranging social repercussions. Young men in the cities were uprooted and isolated, cut off from their traditional social outlets and civic organizations. As a result, loneliness became an epidemic as men found it harder to find mates. This led to a surge of prostitution and illegitimate children. Orphanages were just as much a feature of the early Industrial Revolution as factories, with Oliver Twist-style city scenes playing out every day with increased crime and social decay.

This turbulent trade-off (of increasing GDP at the expense of social stability) was still an on-going factor in the lead-up to World War One. The same Adam Smith who documented the division of labor in "The Wealth of Nations" also warned in the same book that, as countries industrialize, they suddenly require raw materials to make products. If a country doesn't have the requisite supplies of nickel, or iron, or cadmium in their own territory, this leads to the desire for overseas colonies. Since the regions which have these resources are finite, this circumstance naturally leads to conflict as colonial powers vie for the same for overseas territories.

Germany's industrialization provides a perfect case-study. The English felt that Germany's success was coming at British expense. As an example, it might be useful to point out that England, the birthplace of the Industrial Revolution, was still very much tied to the older Mercantile system that preceded Capitalism. In Mercantilism, a country doesn't produce things. Merchants merely sail across the planet, purchase foreign goods at inexpensive prices and re-sell them in the West for a mark-up. In many ways, England's conception of "free market imperialism" was barely different from that of the Roman Empire. They believed in sweat-shops, serfs and colonies.

Germany, by contrast, was using the new capitalistic method of making products domestically by using science rather than slaves. For instance, while England relied on Southeast Asian colonies for rubber tree plants, Germany had raced ahead and invented synthetic rubber using chemistry. The German product was of superior quality and could be made for pennies on the dollar. (Since there was no question of maintaining expensive colonies, Germany could pass the savings onto customers.)

As consumers bought German rubber and England began to lose market-share, grumbling in London began.

In "The Long Twentieth Century," historian Giovanni Arrighi notes, "The United Kingdom exercised world governmental functions until the end of the nineteenth century. From the 1870s onwards, however, it began to lose control of the European balance of power and soon afterwards the global balance of power as well. In both cases, the rise of Germany to world power status was the decisive development."

Business interests appealed to the British government to intercede. They got the ear of the military when it was pointed out that, while Germany had the biggest army in Europe, England had the largest navy. All British might was predicated on this balance of power. But now, within a mere ten-year period, Germany's production of ships had given it the third largest navy in the world.

If England lost ground in this area, they feared that they'd be reduced to an economic backwater as Germany rose into the ascendant.

The British started to conceptualize ways to sabotage German industrial growth. One of these methods was to cut off Germany from petroleum in order to frustrate their ability to fuel their factories. According to William Engdahl, in his book "A Century of War," England was mortified at the prospect of Germany building the Berlin-Baghdad railway which would give them direct access to oil (and allow them to bypass English shipping of petroleum). The British solution to disrupting the new land-based German supply-chain was to create the Serbian nationalist movement. (The trajectory of the new rail-line would take it through Serbia on its way to the Near East, and British tacticians hoped that Serbian nationalists, funded from London, might be induced to obstruct it by any means necessary.)

Engdahl writes, "The rail-link, once extended to Baghdad and a short distance further to Kuwait, would provide the cheapest and fastest link between Europe and the entire Indian subcontinent, a world rail link of the first order.

"From the British side, this was exactly the point. 'If "Berlin-Baghdad" were achieved, a huge block of territory producing every kind of economic wealth, and unassailable by sea-power would be united by German authority,' warned R.G.D. Laffan, at that time a senior British adviser attached to the Serbian Army. 'Russia would be cut off by this barrier from her Western friends, Great Britain and France.'"

As history tells us, the unstable political dynamics of Europe were thrown off-kilter when a Serbian nationalist named Gavrilo Princip shot Archduke Franz Ferdinand. He claimed that he did it in a bid for Serbian independence from the Austro-Hungarian Empire. Although there is evidence that British Intelligence supported the "Black Hand" movement of Serbian separatists for their own geopolitical strategic interests.

Whatever the truth behind the assassination, Germany—bound by treaty to support its ally Austro-Hungaria—lent its support when the Habsburg monarch, Charles I, tried to put down the revolt. England took this opportunity to accuse Germany of helping Austria to suppress democracy and declared war on her on August 4, 1914.

Other Ramifications

The Industrial Revolution did not just have destabilizing domestic effects on England, but also larger geopolitical consequences as it brought them into economic competition and conflict with rival powers. War, it goes without saying, is extremely expensive. English national debt skyrocketed ten-fold as they took out loans to buy armaments. Since their treasury didn't have the ready funds available, they secured financing (mostly from American banks). To make interest payments on the new debt ($38-billion, in today's money), they had to raise taxes on their citizens. Within a single four-year period, the tax rate on the average English citizen went from five-percent to thirty-percent.

To ensure that they would have a ready tax-base among the business sector, the government quashed labor disputes that might thwart economic activity. So they took the unprecedented step of quietly suborning trade unions and labor movements to make sure that factory production wasn't inhibited.

In "The Official History of The Ministry of Munitions," one bureaucrat was quoted as writing in a report, "The progress in equipping our new Armies and also in supplying the necessary war material for our forces in the field has been seriously hampered by the failure to obtain sufficient labour and by delays in the production of the necessary plant, largely due to the enormous demands, not only of ourselves but of our Allies. While the workmen generally, as I have said, have worked loyally and well, there have, I regret to say, been instances where absence, irregular timekeeping and slack work have led to a marked diminution in the output of our factories. In some cases the temptations of drink account for this failure to work up to the high standard expected. It has been brought to my notice on more than one occasion that the restrictions of trade unions have undoubtedly added to our difficulties, not so much in obtaining sufficient labour as in making the best use of that labour."

The British government responded with the Munitions War Act of 1915. It instituted wage controls (as well as a "minimum wage" policy that would be part and parcel of governments ever after).

In "America's Great War," Robert H. Zieger notes that England was not alone in creating these policies and their accompanying regulatory organizations. He writes regarding the United States, saying, "Federal officials took belated and sporadic notice of the special problems and opportunities associated with female employment in munitions and other essential industries creating temporary agencies to monitor women's performance and their reception by employers and co-workers. In a few cases, federal agencies such as the USRA and the NWLB intervened to uphold women's claims for equal pay, access to promotion ladders, and fair treatment in the workplace."

Both countries forced on trade unions so-called dilution agreements that allowed unskilled and semi-skilled workers, including women, to undertake tasks previously reserved for skilled laborers. The agreements were pivotal in increasing production, as they expanded the labor pool and maximized the use of available workforce.

British military historian Hew Strachan explains, "One

solution to the manpower needs of the munitions factories was to 'dilute labor,' to replace skilled workers with unskilled. The greater use of automated processes and the division of production into a large number of distinct, but repetitive, operations permitted such a switch. The principal job of the skilled worker was to maintain the plant that made the arms, not to produce the arms themselves. In Britain the trade unions feared that working methods brought in under the umbrella of wartime necessity would be perpetuated in peacetime and to undermine both their status and their restrictive practices. On 5 March 1915, Lloyd George persuaded both employers and trade unions to accept dilution, but only for the duration of the war and only in the production of munitions. The result was that in Britain, as in France, women were engaged in the manufacture of armaments in disproportionate numbers."

Of course, these changes would not be "just for the duration of the war" (as was promised), and would have long-lasting social repercussions. Not the least of which was the crippling of unions' ability to regulate labor practices and negotiate higher wages for the working-class.

According to "A People's History of the World," by Chris Harman, "By 1917 a British war cabinet report acknowledged that state control had extended 'until it covered not only national activities directly affecting the war effort, but every section of industry.' By the end of the war the government purchased about 90 percent of all imports, marketed more than 80 percent of food consumed at home, and controlled most prices."

This represented an unprecedented expansion of government power and interference in the economy that would later become an enduring feature of modern nation-states.

Another enduring feature that's still with us is the concept of a global central banking system.

After the war, when Germany was saddled by the Allies with crippling reparations payments, certain statesmen like

Woodrow Wilson knew that Germany could never hope to pay it. Strapped with what even the Allies admitted to being unreasonable demands, the German finance minister, Hjalmar Schacht pitched an idea to Montagu Norman, the head of the Bank of England. He envisioned a scheme to create an institution to administer German war reparations. The organization, to be domiciled in neutral Switzerland, would become the central bank of all other central banks around the world. It would be named The Bank for International Settlements.

Adam Lebor, in his book *The Tower of Basel*, writes about the shadowy organization. Despite the Bank for International Settlements being the premier global financial institution, it has evaded publicity and remained solidly outside the public's consciousness. Lebor Writes, "The Swiss authorities have no jurisdiction over the BIS premises. Founded by an international treaty, and further protected by the 1987 Headquarters Agreement with the Swiss government, the BIS enjoys similar protections to those granted to the headquarters of the United Nations, the International Monetary Fund (IMF) and diplomatic embassies. The Swiss authorities need the permission of the BIS management to enter the bank's buildings, which are described as 'inviolable.' The BIS has the right to communicate in code and to send and receive correspondence in bags covered by the same protection as embassies, meaning they cannot be opened. The BIS is exempt from Swiss taxes. Its employees do not have to pay income tax on their salaries."

The bank's first president Gates McGarrah commented in 1931, "The bank is completely removed from any governmental or political control."

History of the BIS

Feeling the pinch of the crushing terms of the *Treaty of Versailles*, Hjalmar Schacht, head of the *Reichsbank*, bristled at the punitive reparations payments demanded by the victors. While the United States counseled moderation, and while England was willing to negotiate, France was belligerent, demanding ever-more money—impossible sums, given Germany's economic position in the rubble after the war.

"Germany was paying its reparations by borrowing from other countries," writes Lebor. "Such a system was no longer feasible. If the Allies really wanted Germany to be able to pay its obligations, the country needed to become productive again. Instead of lending to Germany, the Allies should lend to underdeveloped countries so they could buy their industrial equipment from Germany. Young asked how such a plan could be put into practice. Schacht had a ready answer: by setting up a bank. 'A bank of this kind,' argued Schacht, 'will demand financial cooperation between vanquished and victors that will lead to a community of interests, which in turn will give rise to mutual confidence and understanding and thus promote and ensure peace.'"

Thus what are now called "developing countries" were targeted by the bankrupt economic system after World War One. The plan was to place central banks in each country, and, by extending them credit, have them purchase industrial goods from Germany—after which Germany would remit payment for its reparations obligations.

Since all parties concerned among the advanced economies seemed to benefit, the Schacht plan was put into action and the era of The Economic Hitman commenced.

This is, of course, a reference to John Perkins' book, "Confessions of an Economic Hitman". In the 2004 exposé, he confided about how he, in his capacity as an economic development expert, was dispatched to Third World countries by the international banking system in order to get struggling nations into debt.

Comments Perkins, "I'm haunted by the payoffs to the leaders of poor countries, the blackmail, and the threats that if they resisted, if they refused to accept loans that would enslave their countries in debt, the CIA's jackals would overthrow or assassinate them."

As President John Adams said in 1826, "There are two ways to conquer and enslave a nation. One is by the sword. The other is by debt." Perkins describes this alternate method of war, as alluded to by Adams. In traditional war, armies invade rival countries to steal their resources. In the new paradigm, "war" would be waged by banks. Credit would be the main weapon. Poor countries were offered loans upon the pretext of helping them with costly new infrastructure projects. To receive the loans, the leader of a nation would be asked to put up as collateral his country's natural resources. (If the leader protested that they'd just built a new airport and didn't need another one, he would be offered two choices: Take the loan package, build the unnecessary infrastructure, and ensure that his own family and friends were rich for life. Or try and keep his citizens from being tax-slaves to foreign banks—whereupon "jackals" would be dispatched to assassinate him and replace him with someone willing to plunge his country into debt.) Most leaders, after weighing the options, capitulated. When the respective countries inevitably went into default, the Western banking system would seize their natural resources.

The underpinnings for this system were, needless to say, pioneered by Schacht three-quarters of a century earlier when he and Montagu Norman founded the Bank for International Settlements. He envisioned the Allies using their considerable influence to spread central banks into all the countries of the world. These new banks in developing nations would be "induced" to buy German goods.

After World War Two, new institutions were added to help the Bank for International Settlements achieve these goals. Economist John Maynard Keynes and Assistant US Treasury Secretary Harry Dexter White drafted the blueprints for sister organizations: the World Bank [to provide infrastructure loans for war-torn nations after hostilities ended in 1945, as well as for emerging nations going forward] and the International Monetary Fund [set up with the ostensible goal of stabilizing currencies and promoting economic reform in Third World countries (but in reality to create the institutions in their nations to tax the population to pay for crippling World Bank loans)].

Needless to say, even after Germany's post-war obligations were paid off, the system that was initially created upon the pretext of defraying war reparations continued to spread its tentacles around the world.

In the end, its mandate shifted to creating a new sort of "global federalism," where the sovereignty of individual nation-states was eroded, and a new extra-legal framework was put in place over and above particular countries (analogous to how the federal layer of government was installed over the fifty states in America). Except, the new guiding authority would not be a constitutional branch of government, but a banking system exempt from any law.

The Upshot

In the final analysis, the Bank for International Settlements was a project by Hjalmar Schacht to pay off World War One reparations. That was finally achieved on September 3, 2010, when Germany marked the conclusion of its reparations obligations.

In a perfect world, the Bank would have shut down after its mandate was ultimately achieved.

Sadly, a perfect world eludes us.

Schacht had induced the West's powerful financial elite to help him cushion Germany from its crushing debt by stripmining Third World countries (and installing central banks inside each to help him do so). So, even after the initial reason for setting up this arrangement drew to a successful conclusion, it was too lucrative a scheme to abandon. The money kept flowing in, and the BIS kept getting more powerful.

No one asked why it was continuing to operate—and the small group of eighteen men who run the BIS didn't offer any objections for doing so.

This was one of so many lasting legacies that emanated out from World War One. Another one we will examine hereafter: namely, the innovation of incorporating women into the labor force.

Chapter Two

"This war could not have been fought, either by the other nations engaged or by America, if it had not been for the services of the women,—services rendered in every sphere,— not merely in the fields of effort in which we have been accustomed to see them work, but wherever men have worked and upon the very skirts and edges of the battle itself."

—Woodrow Wilson

In Sir Oliver Lodge's 1916 book "Raymond," where he recounts the death of his son as a result of the war, the grieving author shares some of the letters his late child sent home. In one of them, the younger man recounts all the new words he had heard for the first time on the front. Today, it's hard to believe that, at some point, the word "dug-out" was unheard-of. Raymond Lodge expressed amusement at learning that the new slang term for England was "Blighty," or that "cushy" was a neologism signifying something soft or easy. Another new word to him was "grousing," for "complaining".

For the purposes of this chapter, a then-novel phrase that holds special significance is "the home front". This was coined to metaphorically express how important it was to the war effort to have people back home contributing to the battle. The government began thinking the better of conscripting everybody, because they realized very early on that a person who stays behind and digs coal for the war machine was every bit as important as a soldier on the front lines.

Part of this domestic auxiliary force was women.

In her book "The Hello Girls," Elizabeth Cobbs draws attention to the U.S. Signal Corps and its reliance on females to aid in the war effort. She writes, "The Industrial Revolution had called daughters and wives from their home to fill new jobs. Telephone operating was largely sex segregated. If America was going to position and command its immense forces, it needed women to handle the advanced technologies at which they were expert. They would have to withstand torpedoes, canon fire, influenza, and petty-minded bureaucrats in order to send the word 'over there'."

In a digression, it might be good to take a step back and mull how crucial these women were to the war effort by first conceptualizing the importance of telecommunications.

Historian Duncan Bell, in his book "Dreamworlds of Race," discusses the impact of telecommunications on political states. One reason, for instance, that the British Empire lost hold of its colonial possessions in North America was the geographical distance involved and the difficulty in projecting power over long stretches of space. In 1866 when the first Trans-Atlantic telegraph wire was strung across the ocean, connecting the United States to England, that obstacle was finally overcome. The two nations were now stitched together in a way that had been impossible before. Technology allowed space to shrink and time-zones to melt away as people on opposite sides of the Atlantic could communicate in real-time. Bell comments, "Benedict Anderson argued that one of the principle facilitating conditions of nationalism was the emergence of 'empty homogeneous time' A product (in part) of the technological infrastructure of print capitalism, this sense of temporality allowed a cohesive national community to be imagined as a single unity moving through history."

He adds, "Political thinkers, cultural commentators and scientists alike drew on the language of the nervous system to describe the nature and functioning of the telegraph, just as telegraphic imagery fed into scientific work of the human body. The nervous system metaphor was fused with older organic images of the political community to provide a new account of the body politic: it was animated, controlled, and disciplined by the circulation of electrical pulses carrying information."

Of course, even before the 19th Century, the control of communications by nation-states was seen as crucial. In Antiquity, the "nervous system" of the civilization was the post office. The Persians are the first society of which we have any knowledge, who used a Pony Express-style network to convey correspondence from one point of the empire to another. The Romans would adopt a very similar system, using postal roads to both transact trade and communications, but also as convenient conduits for their troops.

Even as late as the American Revolution, the British held tight reins over the primitive colonial postal system in their American colonies. They inhibited the delivery of newspapers and obstructed the colonies from talking to each other, lest they develop a group-identity. This is one of the reasons why, after the Revolution when the Americans created the U.S. Constitution, they included a provision for a robust postal system, with the construction of the concomitant postal roads.

And make no mistake: The roads themselves are part of the early "nervous system" of a society. In "The Making of the Middle Ages," by R.W. Southern, he comments, "But even in the most favorable geographical conditions, man's technical equipment was so primitive that this helplessness before Nature—which added to his misery in one way—saved him from the misery of organized tyranny. There was a mercifully large gap between the will to rule and the power to do so, and it may be that the bad roads and an intractable soil contributed more to the fashioning of familiar liberties than any other factor at this time."

Winifred Gallagher in her book "How the Post Office Created America" notes the importance of the postal roads in drawing the one-time colonies together into a coherent nation. She adds, "The founders established the post office before they had even signed the *Declaration of Independence*, and for a very long time, it was the U.S. government's largest and most important endeavor—indeed, it was the government for most citizens. This was no conventional mail network but the central nervous system of the new body politic, designed to bind thirteen quarrelsome colonies into the United States by delivering news about public affairs to every citizen—a radical idea that appalled Europe's great powers."

Note, too, how, shortly after World War Two, President Dwight Eisenhower raced to create a new interstate highway system in the United States. It was one of the prerequisites of growing federalism and centralized control of the country. What the citizens perceived as an economic convenience, the emerging Managerial State saw as a crucial part of the control grid in the post-war system. (It provided a stealthy way to bribe states to adopt federal policies in exchange for vast sums of money to maintain the highway.)

But even before World War II—back in World War I—the emerging technology making coordination with the Allies possible was the telephone system.

Without this crucial innovation (which piggybacked on the earlier telegraph network), the United States could never have worked so seamlessly with England and its other confederates in the war. And central to this "central nervous system" were a group of female phone operators working for the U.S. Signal Corps, known colloquially as the "Hello Girls" (a nickname given to them by General "Black Jack" Pershing).

The leader of the unit was a fresh-faced twenty-five year-old woman with chestnut hair and bright blue eyes, named Grace Banker. Having a brother in the 77th Field Artillery, she wanted to do her patriotic duty and aid in the war effort in any way she could. Having a background in "telephony," she wrote the War Office to offer her services.

The U.S. Signal Corps, whose motto was *Pro patria vigilans* ("watchful for the country") wrote her back to request further information. They asked her to forward her educational background, employment history, medical records and a formal photograph, "or a snapshot if good likeness".

While thousands of women applied, only a select few were chosen based on their skills, language proficiency, and ability to handle the rigors of military life. Grace Banker was one of these. She, and the first group of thirty-three women were trained at the AT&T headquarters in New York City. They underwent rigorous instruction to ensure they could perform under the stressful conditions they would face in Europe.

The Hello Girls

When her country was in need, Grace Banker, a Barnard College graduate with a background in languages and a skilled telephone operator, answered the call. Her leadership and technical prowess were instrumental in the unit's success. Banker was known for her calm demeanor, organizational skills, and ability to inspire confidence in her team. She was appointed as the Chief Operator of the Signal Corps Female Telephone Operators Unit, a position that required her to oversee operations and ensure the smooth functioning of communications.

One of the girls under her command was Marguerite Lovera. Born into a French-speaking family in the United States, Lovera grew up bilingual, which made her an ideal candidate for the Signal Corps. She underwent rigorous training, not only in operating the complex switchboards but also in military protocols and the importance of discretion and accuracy in wartime communication.

While Lovera's family were originally from France, another Hello Girl, named Olive Shaw, spoke French due to her father being originally from Quebec, Canada. Unfortunately, he died of heart trouble when she was two years-old, so she fortified her conversational French by speaking with her father's medical assistants. Before the war, she studied at the Sorbonne in France. After the war, she worked as a secretary for Congresswoman Edith Nourse Rogers.

Another prominent figure among the "Hello Girls" was Merle Egan, who brought her own set of skills and determination to the unit. Egan was known for her unwavering resolve and technical expertise. She played a crucial role in managing communications and ensuring that critical messages were relayed accurately and promptly. Her contributions, along with those of her colleagues, were vital to the success of the unit's mission. But it was Egan, who would live till the age of 96, who used her influence to get government recognition for the important unit and to demand a place for them in the official history of World War One.

In early 1918, the "Hello Girls" arrived in Europe, where they were deployed to various locations, including Paris, Chaumont (the headquarters of the American Expeditionary Force), and other strategic points near the front lines. Their primary responsibility was to operate the switchboards that connected calls between different military units and between the AEF and allied forces. This task required not only technical proficiency but also the ability to remain composed under the constant threat of artillery bombardment and other wartime dangers.

The "Hello Girls" were instrumental in maintaining the flow of communication during key military operations. Their work ensured that orders from commanding officers were transmitted without delay, allowing for coordinated efforts on the battlefield. One of the most significant contributions of the "Hello Girls" was their role in facilitating communication during the Meuse-Argonne Offensive, the largest and one of the final campaigns of World War One involving American forces.

One of the most notable aspects of their service was the role they played in connecting important calls between key leaders, including President Woodrow Wilson and British Prime Minister David Lloyd-George. These communications were critical in coordinating strategies and ensuring that the Allied forces could work together effectively.

At the height of the war, they connected 150,000 calls a day. Captain E.J. Wesson commented, "As they assist in the giving of commands concerning artillery direction and calling up of reserves, they have a tremendously responsible position. The morale of the unit is of the finest, and they did not come into it without facing the possibility of danger." Armed with gasmasks and helmets, they worked long hours, often seven days a week.

In "America and the Great War," Margaret E. Wagner makes a penetrating observation. Not only were the "Hello Girls" key to brokering communications between Allied troops, but they also transmitted important information about the Spanish Flu. Wagner writes, "As the Yankee Division assumed its new duties General Peyton C. March, recently returned to Washington from France, where he had been Pershing's artillery commander, was stirring things up at the War Department as the new U.S. Army chief of staff. The General had assumed his duties on Monday, March 4 (as the army was recruiting qualified women to operate the AEF telephone system in France and the War Department was beginning to receive disturbing reports of an unusually virulent flu striking some of the larger stateside training cantonments)."

About sixty of the Hello Girls died during service, mostly from the influenza they were reporting on—which places a spotlight on the dangers of disease. And that opens up a perfect segue to a discussion on the importance of healthcare workers. . . .

Angels in Uniforms: Saving Lives on the Front Lines

Ever since the intrepid image of nursing created by Florence Nightingale in the Crimean War and Clara Barton in the American Civil War, young women entertained romantic images of healthcare workers during international conflicts. So, naturally, they gravitated toward nursing when hostilities erupted in 1914.

The most fashionable outfit for young women that season was a nurse's outfit. As a result, thousands of girls volunteered to be VADs [workers in the Voluntary Aid Detachment]. They raced to take classes on how to set broken bones, dress wounds or cook up beef broth.

As the younger women showed their patriotism in this fashion, the older Aristocracy were not to be outdone. Notable among this demographic was philanthropist Millicent, Duchess of Sutherland, who assembled a host of other dowagers (countesses, all) and arranged a permit to head off to Belgium immediately to attach themselves to the *Secours aux Blessés*.

From her diary we read:

"The Convent of Namur after last week's hurry seemed extraordinarily quiet. Les Soeurs de Notre Dame are scholastic sisters, and they had arranged the school part of the building, which was new and sanitary, as a hospital. My nurses were given a long dormitory where the scholars usually sleep and I had a small dormitory to myself. The nuns treated us most kindly, and said they would do all the cooking for the wounded. In the Belgian Red Cross ambulances and in the military hospital all the nursing is done by partly trained, but willing nuns and ladies. The dressings are done by the doctors.

"It was a strange experience next morning to be sitting in the old Convent garden full of fruit trees and surrounded by high walls, whilst the nuns, the novices, and the postulants flitted about the paths with their rosaries and their little books. It was almost impossible to realise that there were nearly 200 nuns in the Convent so quietly did they move. From an upper window the nurses and I watched a regiment of Belgian artillery roll by. It was coming in from the country. 'A big battle rages near Ramillies,' said one nun. 'All the poor families are coming in in carts.' The Belgian military doctor, Dr. Cordier, came in to inspect our hospital equipment, which only arrived by the last train that reached Namur. . . . He criticised our carbolic, smiled at the glycerine for the hands, and was immensely impressed by our instruments.

"It was almost impossible to find out what was really going on. The noise of the motors, the scout motor cyclists, and the occasional whirr of an aeroplane mingled their sounds with a perpetual clanging of church bells. Our nurses were all busy making splints, cushions, sandbags, etc., and generally getting their scholastic side of the nunnery into one of the finest hospitals in Belgium. The English nuns helped us very much. I shall always remember Sister Marie des Cinq Anges and Sister Bernard.

"On 21 of August there was almost a panic in Namur. All night long the guns had been firing from the forts, and all morning there was hurrying and scurrying into groups of weeping hatless women and of little children. The great secrecy as to all events that were passing filled them with untold fear.

"It was evidently the beginning of s terrible experience. The Germans had been massing on the left bank of the Meuse and had come as close to Namur as circumstances would permit. They had passed through the country carrying off the cattle, burning the villages, cutting the telegraph and telephone wires, and attacking the railway stations. The closeness of the atmosphere had made Namur almost impossible to breathe in, that day. Tired Belgian soldiers came in. They seemed to have so much to wear and to carry. A regiment of Congolais, a Foreign Legion which had been in service in the Congo, marched through with their guns drawn by dogs.

"Never shall I forget the afternoon of 22 August. The shelling of the past hours having suddenly ceased, I went to my dormitory. I had had practically no rest for two nights, and after the emotions of the morning I was falling asleep when Sister Kirby rushed into my room, calling out 'Sister Millicent! The wounded!'

"I rushed down the stone stairs. Six motor cars and as many wagons were at the door, and they were carrying in those unhappy fellows. Some were on stretchers, others were supported by willing Red Cross men. One or two of the stragglers fell up the steps from fatigue and lay there. Many of these men had been there for three days without food or sleep in the trenches.

"In less than 20 minutes we had 45 wounded on our hands. A number had been wounded by shrapnel, a few by bullet wounds, but luckily some were only wounded by pieces of shell. These inflict awful gashes . . ."

But before a single nurse ever reached the Continent, there was an outbreak of infections and diseases back in England. This resulted from poor sanitation and a convergence of troops from the provinces who had little immunity to diseases common to the urban areas. Isolation hospitals were soon overwhelmed with cases of mumps, measles and other illnesses. Overcrowding was such that they soon had to rely on civilian hospitals for the overflow. Young VADs eagerly raced to put their theoretical training into practice as they helped members of the Highland Division or reservists called in from

Wales.

The first nurses wouldn't reach France until the 12th of August, 1914.

Oddly, the atmosphere was initially more festive than fearsome. Before any engagements began, it all had the excitement of a parade—especially as the British Expeditionary Force landed on the coast of France and made their way up to Mons. Local girls followed the troops and handed them flowers. Officers had to keep yelling at villagers and telling them to stop trying to help soldiers in their duties and to cease fraternizing with them.

An American journalist who happened to have purchased a property close to one of the battlefields three months before the war started gave a sense of the idealism that pervaded everything. In her autobiographical book "A Hilltop on the Marne," Mildred Aldrich wrote, "I am old enough to remember well the days of our Civil War, when regiments of volunteers, with flying flags and bands of music, marched through our streets in Boston, on the way to the front. Crowds of stay-at-homes, throngs of women and children lined the sidewalks, shouting deliriously, and waving handkerchiefs, inspired by marching soldiers, with guns on their shoulders, and the strains of martial music varied with the then-popular 'The girl I left behind me,' or 'When this cruel war is over'. But this is different."

She learned just *how* different when she received her first reports from a French youth who told her that there was such pandemonium among the German ranks "as the air was full of flying heads and arms and legs, of boots and helmets, swords and guns that it did not seem as if it could be real—'it looked like some burlesque'; and that even one of the gunners turned ill and said to his commander, who stood beside him: 'For the love of God, colonel, shall I go on?' and the colonel, with folded arms, replied, 'Fire away.'"

What had begun with a circus atmosphere had ended in the

Red Baron's "Flying Circus" (as it was known), whereby enemy aircraft dropped bombs as bodies were atomized by the latest weapons of war.

As for Military Command, they thought they had matters well in hand, with three hospital ships off the coast, additional land-based facilities capable of caring for 7,000 wounded, and an elite corps of nurses (Queen Alexandra's Imperial Military Nursing Service) that had distinguished themselves in the Boer War in 1900.

But when hostilities began in earnest, as superior German forces engaged with less-seasoned British troops, the reality of the situation dawned on everybody. Of 90,000 soldiers who had landed in France, one in six became a casualty. And almost all the wounds developed gas gangrene.

As Captain Geoffrey Keynes, RAMC, commented, "We knew nothing about it at all. Nothing like it had ever been experienced in South Africa on the clean, sandy battleground of the veldt, which had been the army's last experience. Here, on the heavily manured soil of France, it was a different matter. You got this appalling infection with anaerobic bacteria and the men just died like flies. We got the casualties straight from Mons and the infection had usually set in by the time they got to us. If they had compound fractures, full of mud, it was the ideal site for the bacteria to flourish, and, if the men had been several days on the way, as most of them had, the wound was simply a mass of putrid muscle rotting with gas gangrene. Nothing to do with gas as we knew it later in the war. It was called that because the bacillus that grows in the wound creates gas. The whole thing balloons up. You can tap it under your fingers and it sounds hollow. Even with quite a slight wound, when soil and shreds of uniform are carried in by a missile, it starts up. They soon died. We simply didn't know how to treat it. We'd never come across it before. Of course, there were no antibiotics. No effective disinfectants. We would cut away as much of the diseased tissue as we could. On a leg or an arm, we would remove the limb, but that didn't stop it. It just went on up, and still the men would die from the toxic effects of the products of the bacteria. That was the worst thing in the first few months of the war."

After the retreat from Mons, and the equally grueling battles at the Marne and the Aisne, dressing stations popped up like mushrooms all over the countryside as medical staff was mobilized to meet the needs of the Army. Military Command was oftentimes more at home with the Angels of Mercy who were helping, rather than the unruly new group of so-called "Flying Angels" who came in to offer assistance. This was the nickname of the VADs and other wartime nursing organizations that came in with the Territorial Force. (It was always a headache to try and stem the breakdown in discipline that inevitably occurred when young maidens with romantic notions of war came into contact with lascivious soldiers.)

One of these so-called "flying angels" was Sarah Macnaughtan. She belonged to Dr. Henry Munro's Flying Ambulance Corps and was in Belgium in 1914—where she learned the less-romantic side of war.

According to her diary from the fourth of October, we read: "Some fearful cases were brought into us today. My God, the horror of it! One has heard of men whom their mothers would not recognise. Some of the wounded today were among these. All the morning we did what we could for them. One man was riddled with bullets, and died very soon.

"It was awful work. The great bell rings, and we say, 'More wounded,' and the men get stretchers. We go down the long, cold covered way to the gate and number the men for their different beds. The stretchers are stiff with blood, and the clothes have to be cut off the men. They cry out terribly, and their horror is so painful to witness. They are so young, and they have seen right into hell. The first dressings are removed by the doctors—sometimes there is only a lump of cotton—

and the men lie there with their tragic eyes fixed upon one.

"The lights are all off at eight o'clock now, and we do our work in the dark, while the orderlies hold little torches to enable the doctors to dress the wounds. There are not half enough nurses or doctors out here. In one hospital there are 400 beds and only two trained nurses."

According to the book "The British Army and the First World War," by Ian Beckett, Timothy Bowman and Mark Connelly, "Traditionally, the British Army had only employed women as nurses prior to 1914: the trend was continued by Queen Alexandra's Imperial Military Nursing Service (QAIMNS), the Territorial Force Nursing Service (TNS), the Voluntary Aid Detachments (VADs) and the aristocratic First Aid Nursing Yeomanry (FANY). Excluding the 74,000 VADs in 1914, there were over 2,000 other military nurses, a figure that reached over 18,000 by 1918."

Between 1914 and 1921, 20,000 women joined the nursing profession in England. Similar increases were seen in the United States, so that, by the end of World War One, 22,000 nurses had come to the aid of wounded soldiers.

In "A World Undone," by G.J. Meyer, he writes, "More than fifteen thousand women were with the American Expeditionary Force and auxiliary organizations such as the Red Cross by that time. (Ten thousand American nurses had volunteered to serve in the Entente forces before the end of 1914.) The BEF had twenty-thousand nurses and fifteen thousand nurses' aides, the armies of France sixty-three thousand, the Germans ninety-one thousand. They performed magnificently—a hundred and twenty American nurses had died in Europe, and two hundred were decorated for bravery under fire—but they were only a tiny percentage of the women whose lives were affected by four years of war."

In her book "The Second Line of Defense," historian Lyn Dumenil writes, "Like male medicos, they had to learn not to show their horror at the extent of injuries they witnessed and to relentlessly persevere in addressing the needs of their patients. Nursing venues varied, with some stationed at convalescent hospitals and others on special hospital trains or at base hospitals. Small units of medical teams that included nurses also served quite near the front in casualty-clearing stations. With the exception of those stationed at convalescent facilities, most nurses experienced some version of the dramatic spurts of wounded called 'the rush'. Fierce combat produced hundreds of wounded in a short amount of time, and medical staff worked feverishly, often for forty-eight hours straight with little rest. The rush, as Zeiger argues, was much like the soldiers' 'going over the top' and gave nurses a close sense of identity with the battle itself."

"'Hundreds upon hundreds of wounded poured in like a rushing torrent,' an American nurse remembered. 'The crowded twisted bodies, the screams and groans, made one think of Dante's *Inferno*.' Men came in with parts of their face missing, with their sexual organs gone, with limbs reduced to dripping shreds," added historian G.J. Meyer.

Of course, due to the constraints of the time-period, there were more women nurses than women doctors. (In 1918, only about 2% of doctors in England, for example, were female.) Nevertheless, the latter did exist, with Dr. Jane Walker being a notable case. She was on the boards of both the Ministry of Food and Ministry of Munitions. As well as Drs. Louisa Garrett Anderson and Flora Murray, who co-founded the Women's Hospital Corps in London.

According to Susan Grayzel, "The largest medical endeavour completely run by women was that of the Scottish Women's Hospitals (SWH) founded by Dr. Elsie Inglis, a leading Scottish suffragist. The organisation began by launching an appeal through *Common Cause*, the newspaper of the National Union of Women Suffrage Societies (NUWSS), in September 1914 to raise money for medical services that would be offered by women. By the end of

October, sufficient funds had been raised to allow the SWH to create its first hospital in France and later to found several others there and also in Serbia and Russia. Eventually more than a thousand women from all parts of the United Kingdom and its dominions served as doctors, orderlies, nurses, ambulance drivers and other support staff under SWH auspices. These hospitals allowed women to perform medical and surgical work unimaginable in Britain, and the grateful governments of France and Serbia awarded some of these doctors their highest medals."

While working in Serbia, Dr. Inglis wrote on May 30, 1915, "We have had a busy time since we arrived. The Unit is nursing 550 beds, in three hospitals, having been sent out to nurse 300 beds. There is the first surgical hospital, called Reserve No. 3. It was a school, and is in two blocks with a long courtyard between. I think we have got it really quite well equipped, with a fine X-ray room. The theatre, and the room opposite where the dressings are done, both being very well arranged, and a great credit to Sister Bozket [sic] [Sister Boykett].

"There are two other hospitals, the typhus one, No. 6 Reserve [under Drs. Janet McVea, Janet Laird and Catherine Corbett, an Australian], and one for relapsing fever and general diseases, No. 7 Reserve, both barracks. We have put most of our strength in No. 6 and it is in good working order, but No. 7 has had only one doctor [Dr. Elizabeth Brooke], and two day Sisters and one night, for over 200 beds. Still, it is wonderful what those three women have done. We have Austrian prisoners as orderlies everywhere, in the hospitals and in the houses. The conglomeration of languages is too funny for words—Serbian, German, French, English. Sometimes you have to get an orderly to translate Serbian into German, and another to translate German into French before you can get what is wanted. Two words we have all learnt, 'dotra,' which means 'good,' and which these grateful people use at once if they feel a little better, or are pleased about anything, and the other is 'boli,' pain."

And pain there was—especially as the war spread across the Western Front, through Serbia and on into Turkey. As it metastasized, so did disease.

With the heat, insects and rotting bodies, disease claimed almost as many casualties as the weapons. In her book "The Roses of No Man's Land," Lyn MacDonald comments, "Alarmed by the sharp rise in the number of men who had to be evacuated in August and September, the Surgeon General ordered the medical officers of four battalions to examine the men in the line, and the disturbing fact emerged that of these 'fit' men, 50% had 'feeble hearts,' 78 per cent had diarrhea and 64 per cent had sores on the skin. It needed no mathematician to work out that a number of unfortunate soldiers were suffering from all three. When such a man was wounded in the firing line, who could blame a hard-pressed orderly, doing his best to tend to casualties lying packed together on the tiny beaches, swept by shellfire and bullets, exposed to the elements, for failing to slot him into the right pigeonhole? The men were evacuated willy-nilly from the chaos on the beaches on to whatever ship first sailed into the bay."

Due to all the deaths, authorities began referring to these transport vessels as "The Black Ships". The conditions on board were abominable, as Sister Cathy Mellor, attested, "The first night I was on duty in a dysentery ward, and what an experience it was and what hard work, because I had never nursed such cases before. Treatment: keep them clean, diet, rest and Emetine; hypodermic injection of the latter. They soon get into an emaciated condition, enteric is nothing compared to it. In a very short time they look exactly like the babies with summer infantile diarrhoea—those babies who are stricken and die in about forty-eight hours. And how they suffer. It is brutal. I have never seen anything like it.

"They lie there in agony, night and day. Oh, the pity of it all. Great strong men, young, looking as old as men of sixty years. I am not exaggerating at all. Several died while I was there, suffering terribly and conscious up to the last moment. One man from Scotland asked me to write his mother and say, 'Alex was too weak to write'. That was the only message. It struck me as being just about enough to heartbreak her."

The Women's Land Army

Food production is the backbone of any society, as it directly impacts the health, stability, and progress of civilizations. Throughout history, the rise and fall of nations have often been closely linked to their ability to produce and manage food resources. Two significant historical periods—the Late Bronze Age Collapse and the Agricultural Revolution of the Middle Ages—illustrate how food production has influenced the trajectory of human history.

The Late Bronze Age Collapse, which occurred around 1200 BC, was a period of significant upheaval that saw the decline and fall of several advanced civilizations in the Eastern Mediterranean and Near East, including the Mycenaean Greeks, the Hittites, and the New Kingdom of Egypt. In history's earliest-recorded example of "globalization," several empires decided to engage in trade. Without taking regard for the importance of redundancies as a back-up mechanism, they stopped farming and outsourced food production to one country (Egypt). The other trading partners decided to specialize in other areas (like creating bronze weapons or other commercial goods.) This all worked fine until a drought occurred and the one country tasked with producing food was crippled with crop failures. A domino effect of famine and social collapse happened as a result.

Suddenly, societies that had previously thrived on agricultural surpluses found themselves unable to sustain their populations. This food scarcity contributed to social unrest, mass migrations, and the breakdown of trade networks that had previously supported these civilizations. (It had such catastrophic effects that the Greeks forgot how to write for 800 years.) This plunged the Mediterranean into a sustained Dark Age.

In stark contrast to the devastation of the Late Bronze Age Collapse, the Agricultural Revolution in 1300s Europe serves as an example of how innovations in food production can fuel civilizational advancement. Beginning around the 10th century AD, Europe experienced a series of agricultural improvements that dramatically increased food production. Key innovations included the introduction of the heavy plow, the widespread adoption of the three-field crop rotation system, and the use of horse collars and horseshoes, which made plowing more efficient.

These advancements led to significant increases in crop yields, creating surpluses that allowed populations to grow and societies to stabilize. The surplus of food not only fed growing populations but also supported the development of towns and cities, as fewer people were needed to work the land. This shift enabled a portion of the population to engage in other activities, such as trade, craftsmanship, and scholarship, thereby diversifying and strengthening the economy.

The agricultural surpluses generated in the Middle Ages, historians tell us, funded the later Industrial Revolution.

Along with crop rotation and the plow as innovations was the discovery that, by adding nitrates to the soil, crop-yields would expand tenfold.

The search for nitrates, of course, had geopolitical ramifications later on—such as the British Empire taking over the Falkland Islands off the coast of Argentina, in order to harvest its rich deposits of natural fertilizer. They first landed on the island chain in 1690 and had skirmishes back and forth for centuries, up to and including the World War One period and beyond into the 1980s (with the famous Falkland Conflict between England and Argentina).

The Germans had a different solution for harvesting nitrates—namely, extracting it from the air. Eighty percent of the atmosphere that we breathe is made of nitrogen. German scientist Fritz Haber pioneered a method in 1909 to obtain it from the ambient aerosphere. He worked with Carl Bosch to be able to produce nitrates in this fashion at scale, and, by 1913, the Haber-Bosch method was commercialized by German industrial giant BASF.

Historians tells us that, due to the food surpluses that this made available, it saved over a billion lives since the innovation was introduced . . . which provides something of an irony, owing to the fact that, just months after it hit commercial markets, World War One began (which brought farming to a stand-still).

"The war drained millions of men from the land," wrote H.P. Willmott. "On small family farms, women and grandfathers and children coped as they have always coped in times of crisis, and shouldered the extra burden themselves. In France, the drop in food production was compounded by German occupation, and was so serious that by 1917 the government had released 300,000 soldiers from the army to work on the land. Forced labor was the German government's solution to the land crisis, and by 1918 100,000 Belgians and 600,000 Poles were at work on German farms and factories. In Britain women were asked to take the place of men who had been diverted from agriculture. The first official government-sponsored organization was the Women's Forage Corps, founded in 1915, and this was followed by the Women's Forestry Corps and the Women's Land Army."

Regarding the Women's Forage Corps, it was led by Mrs. Atholl Stewart, who held the title of Superintendent of Women. Working in gangs of six, females under her command oversaw all things related to horse-transport of food: for instance, hay-making, sewing tarpaulins, mending sacks, and so forth. Though civilians, they were given quasi-military uniforms consisting of a khaki overcoat, dark green breeches, black boots and gaiters. Emblazoned on their brass shoulder insignia were the initials "FC" (for Forage Corps).

The superintendant answered to Brigadier-General Hill Godfrey Morgan, and it was run as if it were a special project of the army.

The program was so successful that they expanded it in March of 1917, creating the Women's Forestry Corps, and, a month before that, the Women's Land Army.

According to Stephen and Tanya Wynn, in "Women in the Great War," the Women's Land Army was formed by Meriel Talbot, and the two authors add, "Women, aged 18 or older, had to initially undergo four weeks of training, and by the very nature of the work, needed to be physically fit. They became affectionately known as 'land girls' and looked after livestock, including horses, sheep, pigs and cattle. They milked cows and undertook general manual labour on the farms."

Eventually, 113,000 women took up agricultural work in Britain. As Napoleon Bonaparte said, "An army marches on its stomach". Without these brave and tireless females, military efforts would have ground to a stand-still—to say nothing of the wider society, which relied on food to maintain public health and social order.

At the start of World War One, Great Britain imported two-thirds of all its food. With German U-boats creating blockades, food security became a serious issue with the government rationing meat, sugar, fat and a host of other items, while rendering it illegal to export foodstuffs. In point of fact, by the time America entered the war in 1917 Great Britain was estimated to have had only six weeks left of food. So the efforts of all the brave women working under the Ministry of Food, or other related programs such as the Women's Land Army shouldered a heavy (and important) burden.

Munitions Factories

War requires weapons. Britain saw its production of explosives, for instance, go from 24,000 tons in 1915 to almost 186,000 tons by 1917. The German production of explosives was even more exaggerated, rising tenfold between 1914 and 1917. All this increased demand required the repurposing of factories.

Consequently, industrial plants that once produced consumer goods such as clothing, household items, and other non-essential products either closed or converted their operations to support the war effort. This led to widespread unemployment among female workers in civilian industries, prompting a significant migration towards munitions factories. By 1917, there were about a million workers in the munitions industry in England, 90% of whom were women.

According to "Secret Warriors," by Taylor Downing, "The expansion of these new munitions factories was rapid and required a small army of workers to operate them. With so many men needed at the front, many of the recruits were young women who flocked in to take up the new jobs. Photographs show vast factory floors with rows of women pouring chemicals into shell casings. By the end of the war 947,000 women were working in munitions factories across Britain, becoming popularly known as 'Munitionettes'. Many of them came from textile mills where women had traditionally been employed in factory work, but, to quote one report at the time, 'they came also from Scottish fishing villages, from Irish bogs, and the workrooms and villas of English provincial towns.' There was a crisis for the middle classes with the sudden lack of servants as so many women left domestic service to take up better-paid work in the factories."

In "The First World War," by Hew Strachan, he concurs with this pattern, writing, "In 1914 7.7 million French women already had jobs, and they made up 32 per cent of the total workforce; by the war's end they accounted for 40 per cent of the workforce. In Britain women workers rose from just under 6 million, or 26 per cent of the workforce, to just over 7.3 million, or 36 per cent in the same period. In Germany the number of females in insured employment expanded so quickly in the two decades before the war that the increase during the war, from about 3.5 million to just over 4 million, represented a decline in the rate of growth. Germany makes very evident the pattern that prevailed elsewhere, too: that those who entered munitions production did so from other occupations; the war caused working-class women to change jobs more than it brought women into the workplace."

In "A World Undone," by G.J. Meyer, he corroborates this, writing, "As many of the factories were shut down, 60 percent of those women were thrown out of work. Sixty-seven percent of garment industry jobs disappeared in France and elsewhere many of the women who went into the munitions factories were no doubt motivated by patriotism. But for many it was also a matter of survival."

The working environment was nerve-wracking. Not only were the women in constant fear of German Zeppelins (whose targets the factories were), but they handled extremely dangerous and volatile substances. A moment's inattention and calamity would strike. Because of this, the conditions were naturally demanding, characterized by strict discipline and rigorous schedules. Women often worked 10-hour shifts, six days a week, with few breaks. The intense labor and lack of adequate rest took a toll on their health, leading to chronic fatigue and other health issues.

Because of the intense pressure to meet quotas, safety

inspections were often not as rigorous as they could have been—resulting in disasters such as:

- The White Lee Chemical Works (a subsidiary of the Henry Ellis Acid Works), where, on 2 December 1914, ten people were killed.
- Low Moor Chemical, where, on 21 August 1916, thirty-eight were killed.
- Barnbow Munitions Factory, where, on 5 December 1916, thirty-five women were killed.
- Hooley Hill Rubber and Chemical Works, when on 13 June 1917, forty-six fatalities occurred.

There were, of course, many, many more such incidents—most hidden by wartime censorship.

Jessica Lozier Payne was a journalist for the *Brooklyn Daily Eagle* who wrote a first-hand account at the time. She commented for her readership, "Among all the changes which the war has caused in industry none has been more spectacular than those brought about by the ever-increasing demand for shot and shells. In the many new employments for women it is the munition story that is the wonderful one.

"The government called on every machine shop and foundry in the United Kingdom to turn out munitions. In addition, old warehouses were hastily fitted with lathes and tools and new buildings run up and equipped as speedily as possible. Where were the workers to be found? The men were needed at the front and there was nothing for it but to call upon the women to do their bit and serve their country and their flag. A tremendous army of women was needed to serve as machine hands, and no readier patriotism has been shown than the way in which they responded to the call. By the thousands they came trooping in and are still coming, although the tide has swelled beyond the quarter of a million mark.

"In Edinburgh I was eager to see and talk to these women munition workers, but it is very difficult to get on the inside of these plants doing government work, for naturally they do not desire visitors.

"But through the influence of friends, who vouched for my innocuousness, an appointment was made for me to visit the works of Bruce, Peebles & Co., the largest engineering works in Scotland, and now employing 150 girls on munition work, and also the shops of David Thomson, engaged before the war in manufacturing bakery machinery, but now doing nothing but government work and employing over 200 girls.

"Entering Bruce, Peebles & Co. I found myself surrounded by the hum and throb of speeding machinery. Long aisles of electrically driven tools, each with a woman worker before it absorbed in her task. There were many young girls, pretty and rosy cheeked, and all dressed in a uniform of lavender cotton goods which completely covered them, and on their heads were shirred mob caps of the same to keep their hair from dust and from being caught in the machinery. The age seemed to range from 18 to 25, and they seemed very interested when the forewoman told them that I was a lady from America who wanted to see the women working.

"I spoke to one smiling, blue-eyed girl, whose tool was making grooves in a core. She had only one part of this operation to complete, and it did not require special skill, since the tool was set to perform this task automatically.

"'Don't you get tired of doing this ten hours every day?' I asked her.

"'No, I like to watch my tool cut the metal, just as if it were cheese, and every shell I pass along I say, 'there goes another for our boys at the front.'

"That seems to be the spirit that carries the work along, and you can feel it as you walk by these rows of women, each faithfully doing her bit to help, for, without doubt, every woman there had some man belonging to her out on the fighting line.

"The heaviest work I saw women doing was operating the hydraulic press, which, under tremendous pressure, welds the copper band on the shells. Three young Amazons were doing this and were jesting and laughing and apparently enjoying it.

"The government inspectors were young women, too, and had instruments for measuring each shell before it was passed for test. Those that did not come up to requirements were rejected."

In "The First World War: A Complete History," by Martin Gilbert, he says, "Women were already working in enormous numbers in munitions factories throughout Britain. Long hours, acrid fumes and low pay were among the negative features of the work, but the patriotic call for volunteers was as strong as for soldiers." But he adds somberly, "Death also came by accident to those who were helping the war effort. On April 2, an accidental explosion at a munitions factory in Faversham in Kent killed 106 munitions workers, many of them women."

In the book "On Her Their Lives Depended," Angela Woollacott comments on the lives of munitions workers, saying, "When they sought their own agency to control and shape that experience to their own ends, however, they were harshly and publicly condemned, were considered threatening by male coworkers, and were widely criticized for exhibiting autonomy in their social behavior and the ways they chose to spend their increased income. They were accused of sexual promiscuity, drunkenness, and wanton extravagance and were subjected to the surveillance of newly created women police forces."

Police Forces

The war created an unprecedented demand for public service, prompting women to step into roles vacated by men who had gone to fight. Among these roles was the formation of voluntary women's patrols, a pioneering effort in female law enforcement and social work.

The Voluntary Women's Patrols (VWPs) were initially established by the National Union of Women Workers (NUWW) in 1914. The primary objective was to address concerns about the welfare and moral behavior of women, especially young women, who were perceived to be at risk of moral corruption in the absence of male supervision. The VWPs aimed to maintain public order, offer guidance, and protect women from exploitation and vice.

The patrols were made up of volunteers who were trained in basic policing skills, first aid, and social work. They operated in various public spaces, such as parks, railway stations, and entertainment venues, where they would monitor and assist women and children. Their presence was intended to deter immoral behavior and provide a reassuring presence in the community.

The training of VWP members was relatively comprehensive, given the volunteer nature of the force. Training programs included instruction in self-defense, first aid, and an understanding of legal procedures. Members were also educated on social issues such as the dangers of venereal disease and the importance of maintaining moral standards.

Organizationally, the VWPs were structured similarly to conventional police forces, with ranks and a chain of command. This structure helped instill discipline and ensured that patrols operated efficiently and effectively. The NUWW played a central role in coordinating these efforts, providing oversight, and ensuring that patrols adhered to their guidelines.

The primary role of the VWPs was to patrol public spaces and ensure the safety and moral conduct of women and children. However, their responsibilities extended beyond mere surveillance. Patrol members often engaged in social work, providing assistance to women in distress, offering guidance on employment and housing, and intervening in cases of domestic abuse.

One of the key areas where VWPs made a significant impact was in the supervision of "khaki fever," a term used to describe the excitement and behavior of young women enamored with soldiers. VWPs worked to mitigate the potential for inappropriate relationships and the spread of venereal diseases, which were significant concerns for public health and military efficiency.

One of these controversial measures was the imposition of curfews, often enforced with the help of Voluntary Women's Patrols. These curfews aimed to reduce the potential for disorder and to curb the spread of venereal diseases among soldiers, which was a significant concern for the military authorities.

(When the Americans eventually came into the war in 1917, 259,612 were infected—which accounted for 5% of the enlisted men. General Pershing, who had himself had gonorrhea when he was a young man, took active steps to dissuade conscripts from visiting prostitutes, such as requiring soldiers to check in at night to hamper their efforts to go to red light districts, as well as having regular inspections of genitals, which were euphemistically called "short arm inspections". They set up "vice-free zones" around military bases or encampments. Any women roaming the vicinity with illicit intent were rounded up and sent to reformatories or detention centers.)

England had similar policies in place. Curfews were implemented in towns with large troop presences to limit the soldiers' opportunities for engaging in activities that could lead to the spread of venereal diseases. The men were required to return to their barracks or billets by a certain time each evening, reducing their chances of visiting brothels or engaging in casual encounters that could result in infections. These measures were part of a broader effort to maintain the health and readiness of the troops.

One of the key legal instruments used to address the issue of venereal disease was contentious Regulation 40d under the Defense of the Realm Act (DORA). DORA, enacted in 1914, granted the government extensive powers to ensure public safety and national security during the war. Regulation 40d specifically targeted the transmission of venereal diseases by making it an offense for a person to knowingly infect another person. This regulation was primarily aimed at women, as they were often blamed for the spread of these diseases.

Under Regulation 40d, "women of ill-repute" could be arrested and subjected to medical examinations. If found to be infected, they could be detained and treated. This regulation was highly controversial, as it was seen as discriminatory and an infringement on personal liberties. Many women's organizations and suffrage groups protested against it, arguing that it unfairly targeted females and did little to address the behavior of the men who were also responsible for spreading the infections.

Outside of the narrow bandwidth of that solitary policy, the VWPs had a profound impact on British society during World War I. Their presence and activities helped to maintain social order during a time of great upheaval and uncertainty. By addressing issues of moral conduct and public safety, they contributed to the broader war effort by ensuring that communities remained stable and supportive of the war effort.

Moreover, the VWPs played a crucial role in changing perceptions about women's capabilities and roles in law enforcement. Their successful operation demonstrated that women could perform tasks traditionally reserved for men, paving the way for greater acceptance of women in public service roles.

The end of World War I did not mark the end of the VWPs. The success and necessity of their work led to the establishment of more formal women's police units in the post-war period. In 1918, the British government officially recognized the contribution of women to policing by forming the Women Police Service (WPS), which included many former VWP members.

The experience gained by these women during the war proved invaluable in the development of women's roles in law enforcement. The establishment of the WPS marked a significant step forward in the integration of women into the police force, setting a precedent for future developments in gender equality in public service roles.

Women in Transportation

In the United Kingdom, the transportation sector saw one of the most significant shifts in female employment. With a large number of men conscripted into the military, women stepped into roles that had been exclusively male. The London General Omnibus Company, for instance, began employing women as conductors and drivers. By the end of the war, around 100,000 women were working in roles directly related to transport, including as bus conductors, tram drivers, and in railway services.

The Women's Army Auxiliary Corps (WAAC) was another critical development. Established in 1917, the WAAC included sections dedicated to motor transport. Women in the WAAC worked as drivers, mechanics, and clerks, supporting the British Army both at home and on the front lines. Their work was vital in maintaining the efficiency and effectiveness of the military's transport operations.

But Britain was not alone. In France, which bore the brunt of much of the war's devastation, women also stepped into critical roles within the transportation industry. The French Army employed women as drivers and ambulance operators, roles that required not only technical skill but also immense courage under fire.

One of the most famous women to take up such a role was Marie Marvingt, a pioneering French aviator and mountaineer. During the war, she served as an ambulance driver at the front, and her contributions were recognized with numerous awards. Additionally, women were employed in public transportation roles, such as tram conductors in Paris, as the war effort necessitated their participation in keeping the country moving amidst the chaos.

The United States, entering the war later in 1917, also saw women take on roles in the transportation industry. While the U.S. had a smaller scale of female involvement compared to Europe, it was nonetheless significant. Women began working as streetcar operators, truck drivers, and even in the railroad industry.

In Germany, women also entered the transportation industry, albeit under more restrictive conditions. The German government, facing a severe shortage of labor as the war dragged on, began employing women in roles such as tram conductors and railway workers. However, the social acceptance of women in these roles was more limited compared to other countries due to Germany's attitude that women should be occupied with *"kinder, kirche, küche"* [children, church and cooking].

Despite these limitations, women in Germany contributed significantly to the war effort through their work in transportation. Their involvement, though often overlooked, was crucial in keeping the home front functioning and ensuring that goods and resources were transported where they were needed most.

Among prominent women who made their mark in transportation was Olive May Kelso King, who was an Australian who volunteered as an ambulance driver in France and later in Serbia. Her courage and dedication made her a legendary figure in the field. King purchased and modified her own ambulance, which she named "Ella the Elephant," and drove it through some of the most dangerous areas of the war. Her efforts saved countless lives, and she was awarded numerous honors for her service.

A journalist named Ruth Wright Kauffman reported on women ambulance drivers in France for *The Outlook* magazine. Her piece appeared October 3, 1917, wherein she wrote, "It's a dusty business riding at a good clip in an ambulance for twenty or thirty miles on one of those long white French roads—the kind they have so much poetry about. I was glad I wasn't a stretcher case—but let me tell you how it happened.

"I was to be driven by the only sort of conveyance in that part of the world to a large military hospital in Northern France. The only sort of conveyance was an ambulance.

"I waited at base headquarters until I saw the great gray creature with its scarlet cross pull up on the other side of the street. For a moment I thought that the driver, who walked toward me in a motor cap and rubber coat and high boots, must be a man, and stocky and alert and somewhat young man. Then I saw my mistake.

"'You're to come with me, I think,' she said, holding out a strong hand. 'Wait a minute, please. I've kept the cushions doubled over, so they wouldn't get dusty, but I shall have to dust them, after all. I hope you don't mind not starting for another hour. I've a lot of calls to make.'

"I did not mind. But I was glad that she invited me to go with her while she made them. None the less, I took my place gingerly within the ambulance. I had never stepped inside an ambulance before, and this one, which had carried so many wounded soldiers, four by four—the last batch only yesterday—made me hold back for an instant.

"My driver delivered her messages here and collected her mail there, slinging, without the slightest hesitation, heavy bags of it that would have been beyond my strength. Soldiers saluted her, but she was left alone to hoist boxes and big sacks. She wasted no time, her manner was businesslike, and she performed her errands with military precision.

"For the first half of the trip I stayed back with an over-age Red Cross man, who spent his time hunting up missing soldiers and questioning the wounded for details of their comrades. There were two other passengers—two rosy-cheeked young women in the V.A.D. (Volunteer Ambulance Drivers) uniform that one comes soon to recognize, returning from a fortnight's leave to England. They were bubbling over with chatter of their holiday, and were anticipating seeing their old friends again. They had been doing Red Cross work in France for over a year, and were practical enough not to look on the dark side of their clouds. They reminded me more of school-girls returning after holidays than anything else, for they must have been very young.

"Then, for I was white from the dust sucked up from the road, I changed to a seat beside the driver, where she thought it might be cleaner.

"We moved at top speed and rattled over all the back roads while we executed our various official orders. We passed numbers of German prisoners. A group of three of them smiled good-morning to us. I saw a Tommy give a light to another German. My driver told me that she had driven many Germans to and from the hospital, but it made no apparent difference to her; they were wounded when she had to do with them.

"She was looking forward to the summer, and called my attention to the luxuriant Lombardy poplars and the masses of flowers that miraculously grew and kept in order: roses that hung over walls, huge clusters of peonies. Not that it would have any effect on the amount of work. The hospital had always been full since she arrived, although there had been depressing occasions when it had suddenly become crowded to twice its capacity; but summer meant easy weather conditions, and motor-drivers perforce consider the weather conditions. The winter had been incredibly cold. For the nursing members, who lived in practically unheated huts, it must have been almost unbearable; but what could be done when there was a shortage of fuel? The drivers had a charming house set in a lovely garden. It used to belong to a French Deputy. In winter, however, it was conspicuous for its single open fireplace, around which eighteen girls could not comfortably toast themselves.

"'There's one good thing about that,' I was cheerfully told. When you're kept pretty cold all the time, you don't feel the outside cold nearly so much. Most of our work this winter had a way of coming along between two and three o'clock in the morning. Now that it's fine weather and makes no difference, the trains generally arrive about six. It's perverse of them!'

"There had been snow for long periods from November until April, sometimes several feet deep. My driver had once run into a drift during a storm and stuck there. Fortunately, she was quite alone at the time. She had walked back, got another ambulance, returned to find the snow so banked up that there was no digging her first car out, and she finally had to tow it home. She has now made it a rule never to go out without a shovel.

"I wondered if she had to know much about mechanics.

"'Well, you see,' she explained, 'I had my own car and had been running it for five years, so I had no trouble in qualifying. I can do any road work, but I'm not a skilled mechanician. I mean, if the car completely broke down it would have to go to the garage for repairs. Several men are kept there to attend to the more serious troubles.'

"'Do you have to take up Red Cross work before you qualify as a driver?' I asked.

"'Yes, now. But I was in the original lot, so I've never taken a course in Home Nursing or First Aid. It wasn't required then. Now they had to take courses both in First Aid and in motor-driving. The First Aid is very important. We never have an orderly with us, you know, and when we come this way it's about twenty miles. We've often had to transfer men when they were really in too dangerous a condition to be moved, so as to make room for incoming train-loads, and it's rather awful not to know what to do if one of them faints or has a hemorrhage.'

"'You don't carry them at this pace, do you?' I gasped.

"'We crawl,' she laughed.

"'I suppose pulling down that flap at the rear keeps out the dust?'

"'No; not a bit. There doesn't seem to be any way to avoid the dust. Sometimes the stretcher cases have dust all over their eyelids when we get them to the end of the journey.'

"In the town itself—a town once overflowing with summer tourists from all parts of the world, and gaily picturesque with its mixture of old France and new, with its hotels and golf and tennis and white cliffs and sands where the brightly dressed children used to play—I saw first the lolling soldiers in their blue invalid uniforms on the promenade by the sea, their figures silhouetted against a brilliant sky. Casino [*sic*] and hotels are now hospitals, but for a space I lost sight of that side of things and, with the gracious permission of the commanding officer, I was taken to see the motor-drivers' headquarters and their immaculate garage.

"The officer under whom the girls directly work showed me, with an air of pride, the fourteen cars.

"'Each girl has her own ambulance,' he said, as he pointed them out one by one; 'and she takes entire care of it herself. There are no night shifts, so she must be ready for duty at any time within the twenty-four hours at a few minutes' notice. Generally, the girls are working here the better part of each morning, except that two or three of the cars are nearly always on the road. The duties consist in a good deal more than transporting the wounded. The drivers are under orders to go whenever they are sent, wherever they are sent, for whatever purpose they are sent, and that means carrying mails, bringing passengers, collecting stores, concert parties—anything that must be brought or transferred. The girls never complain. I've never heard one say she was tired. And the ambulances are kept in much better condition than when the men had them—we are forced to admit that. The girls take a pride in them, you see.'

"I pointed to a toy monkey perched in front of one ambulance.

"'Oh, that's a mascot. They all like mascots. Curious, isn't it? You'll be going back with that car, I expect.'

"At the Deputy's house we came upon the girls eating lunch, a sturdy-looking assemblage, their faces ruddy from the winds, their eyes spirited, their whole bearing enthusiastic. As most of them had held their jobs for at least a year, the newness and adventure of their work had worn off. They were not in France through any war hysteria. One girl said to me that after three months comes the hardest strain; for by that time you are sick of just the same roads and the same stones day in and day out. Afterwards you get used to it and forget the monotony.

"'Don't a lot of you break down?' I asked.

"'No; surprisingly few. One girl went home to-day because the doctor thought she wasn't fit. The winter was pretty hard on her. But we're all strong to begin with, and of course we have a severe medical examination before we are accepted. We're supposed to have nothing to do besides driving, though in the end we do a great many other things, because nobody is within reach, and things that must be done must be done at once.'

"'What do you do when work's over?'

"'We never know when it's over! That's the worst of it. You can't count on the hour when anything's going to happen in a war. If the Germans wound our men, and there's a train-load to come, we must be there. We have a regular route to and from the station, so we never get in one another's way. For instance, yesterday, we brought the entire four hundred and fifty men—and they were mostly lying cases—in an hour and a half. The first train was unloaded and deposited at the casino in twenty-eight minutes, but we were delayed by the second train; they generally arrive in two sections.'

"'How long does it take to bring in one load from the local station?'

"'Six or seven minutes. But the return trip takes no time; we shoot along with the empties.'

"'But,' I persisted, 'It isn't only driving these ambulances that keeps you looking so well.'

"'Oh, no,' said another driver, the most rosy-cheeked of all, I think. 'We're great believers in exercise and open air. Whenever we get a moment off, we go out. Tennis and walking and golf and bathing when it's at all safe. There's a swift current, and we're not allowed to bathe without a boat. We never go so far away that we can't be found quickly. That's the really hard thing, that awful feeling of responsibility. But we do manage to take a lot of exercise. And then we don't worry. It's a rule not to worry.'

"In the beginning the girls had come as a unit of fourteen motor-drivers only. They were the pioneers, for this was the first place in France where women ambulance-drivers were used, and one can well-imagine the struggle that must have ensued with the military authorities before they could be persuaded that women were as capable as men for driving ambulances. For some months this unit of fourteen did its own cooking and housekeeping in odd leisure moments; but the odd moments were few and far between. The girls had no energy left to cook and keep house, so finally the unit was increased to consist of eighteen members, including two cooks, a housemaid and a parlor-maid—all voluntary. The unit is on half government rations and receives enough money to pay for laundry. Tickets to England for the semi-annual fortnightly leave are provided, but in the end the girls are out of pocket, because they buy some of their food. A great deal of the food they receive is tinned, as if they were soldiers; and tinned butter, I can well believe, is more than one can pleasantly endure.

"My return journey—in the ambulance with the monkey— showed an instance of skill. We had barely entered the town of our destination when one of the tires collapsed. In five minutes exactly, without any fuss, but with the usual idle crowd that collects in a country at war as well as in a country at peace, a fresh tire was in place and we were again on our way.

"What, I think, made me see most clearly into the lives of these girls was a sort of diary, kept in very brief form, into which their commandant let me take a glimpse. It gave me what the spoken words could not of themselves give, and showed, through its very lack of intent to show, the rare courage of these young women, set among conditions that not so long ago would have been considered impossible for women to bear, especially as these motor-drivers belong to a class that have never dreamed of earning their living, and were certainly unused to hardships before they 'signed on' for their present work. The bald statements of fact from the diary are the more poignant because they are expressed as mere commonplaces. I quote bits lifted here and there, without dates:

"'*The rush of work for this unit began on Sunday and continued roughly ten days. All the unit without exception worked splendidly, and besides being many hours on the road kept their cars in such excellent condition that, in spite of hard usage, not a car suffered from neglect.—and—joined the unit to assist with housework, as all the drivers were wanted. Within the fortnight we carried 2,115 lying cases, 719 sitting cases. The mileage was 8,718 miles. . . .*

"'*In one day two ambulance trains were evacuated and three hospital ships were loaded. . . .*

"'*The latter half of the last fortnight has been very busy. The trains have been met, and, though the men have not been able to be evacuated to England, . . . large numbers of sitting cases have been carried by the convoy to convalescent camps. The garage has been converted into a temporary hospital, and the cars are at present parked on the square. Several members of the unit have volunteered to help with the patients in the garage, and their offer has been very gratefully accepted by the matron, as the increased number of beds has been a great strain on the nursing staff. The assistance rendered in getting patients' meals, cutting up dressings, making beds, etc., by the unit, especially by those who hold the Home Nursing certificates, has been most appreciated.*

"'The weather has been intensely cold, and it has been difficult to prevent the cars from freezing during the night. . . .

"'Transport has been difficult owing to the state of the roads, which in places have been several feet thick in snow. On more than one occasion drivers have had to dig their cars out of the drifts. . . .

"'Repairs have been heavy, and have been done by the unit themselves. Most of the evacuations have taken place in the night, and this has frequently entailed a full day's work in the workshop being followed by a night on the road. Notwithstanding this, the health of the unit is excellent. . . .'

"What struck me most was the fact mention was made of the possibility of the cars freezing, while nothing was said of hands or feet. That is the essential quality of these drivers; they are so much more distressed over their individual ambulances than over their personal discomforts.

"I mentioned this to the commandant.

"'Well, I don't' know,' she said, smiling deprecatingly. 'When we had that huge lot of fifteen hundreds instead of our nine hundred and fifty capacity, we were pretty sleepy. I don't know about most of the girls, though they couldn't have had it any easier than I did; I know that I got only three and a half hour's sleep in forty-eight hours, and as for food, I seized what I could when I saw it. We didn't need much rocking after that stretch of work was over.'

"And the colonel in command, who won his Victoria Cross under heavy fire in the South African War long before the tradition of keeping women out of affairs military had been broken, confessed to me:

"'I should feel a lot safer with those young women than with most men.'"

WAACS

Another pivotal social change that was inaugurated by World War One was the identification of women with clerical work. Prior to World War One most "secretaries" were men. After The Treaty of Versailles, when the term was uttered it invoked a new feminine connotation that it had never previously had. This arose in part because of the WAAC program (Women's Army Auxiliary Corps). This was inaugurated on 28 March 1917, after a report written by Lieutenant General Sir Henry Lawson after the disastrous Battle of the Sommes, which took place from July to November, 1916. More than a million soldiers died, with British casualties amounting to 420,000 (including 125,000 deaths).

To free up more men to fight, Lawson suggested using women as reserve forces, displacing men in administrative positions. He initially envisioned sending an initial 12,000 women to France (though eventually this would swell to 57,000). They wanted this new organization subdivided into four sections: 1) mechanical/technical, 2) cookery, 3) labor (including ordnance), and 4) communications and clerical.

Each unit would have twenty women for each officer. Although to stress that the women were not officially in the military (but only volunteers) they refused to use military ranks. The women in charge were known as controllers or administrators. Underneath them in the taxonomy were officials, forewomen, assistant forewomen and workers.

Lawson was adamant that women should run all the departments. His choice to oversee the WAAC division was Alexandra Mary Chalmers Watson. She was the first woman to receive a medical degree from the University of Edinburgh. Through her mother's side, she was also related to the first woman to qualify as a doctor in England, Elizabeth Garrett Anderson. She was also the older sister of Auckland Campbell Geddes, 1st Baron Geddes. He was a member of David Lloyd George's coalition government. Because of her political connections and organizational competence, she was thought the perfect choice to be the chief controller of the new initiative. The only problem was that she had a new family and was disinclined to take the position, given the fact that it would require her to live in France for extended periods of time.

Such was their desire to keep her that they created a deputy controller position, who would act as her surrogate on the Continent. They allowed her to choose the woman who would fill this position. She chose Helen Gwynne-Vaughan. The latter was born Helen Fraser, from a multi-generation military family (with her own father being Major Francis Edward Fraser). She became a scientist and married a distinguished botanist named David Gwynne-Vaughan who died in 1915. Even before she had been widowed, she yearned to engage in service to her nation during the war. So she initially joined the VADs. But, no sooner had she signed on, than she had to withdraw in order to nurse her ailing husband. After his subsequent death, she made her intentions known (after a suitable mourning period) that she wanted to donate her energies to whatever patriotic cause presented itself. At just that moment, Alexandra Chalmers Watson reached out to her to ask if she'd like the newly-created deputy controller position. She jumped at the chance and threw herself into the job, performing with exceptional competence.

It was largely through Gwynne-Vaughan's efforts that the practical aspects of the WAAC organizational structure came into being. It was she who oversaw the creation of subdivisions that organized female mechanics, munitions workers, cooks, and most importantly clerical staff.

No sooner was she in France than the Army was demanding that she send women to act as censors, redacting the letters of German POWs. Likewise they handled other communications (comparable to the "Hello Girls" from America), as well as running the postal service.

Critical to Allied war efforts was censorship, and controlling the postal system allowed them to steam open letters and control flows of information.

And the control of flows of information leads us into our next section, on spies . . .

Chapter Three

In the book "Female Intelligence," by Tammy Proctor, she remarks, "When across Europe war was declared in 1914 and again in 1939, and with the advent of a perpetual militarized state during the Cold War, the rapidly ballooning bureaucracies of the secret state needed women's power. In short, without the exploitation of cheaper female labor, the British government could not have created the vast networks of surveillance that yielded hundreds of thousands of pages detailing the activities of enemy aliens, domestic dissidents, and suspected spies between 1914 and 1918. The modern system of counterespionage and secrecy in Britain was built and organized partly through the labor of women employed during the Great War."

So just as the First World War led to a modern world where central banks wield unprecedented power over nations, so it also left us with the modern security state.

Interestingly, the origins of the intelligence agency go back to a woman: namely, Queen Elizabeth I in England. She called it her "Secret Service". It was administered by her spymaster (and Prime Minister) William Cecil, and run by Sir Francis Walsingham back in the 1500s. Spies back then were referred to as "intelligencers". After the Protestant Reformation, when England declared that the monarch would now displace the Pope as head of the Church, a situation emerged where Queen Elizabeth was her nation's chief executive as well as its spiritual leader. As a result, the Church became an instrument of State power. Protestant parishioners were pressed into service to gather intelligence, spy on Catholics, and to pass on any information of plots against the Queen back to The Secret Service.

In its earliest incarnation, the Puritans doubled as spies. (They lost favor, however, when they declared that the messiah had come in the form of William Hackett in 1591. They asserted that the Queen had been deposed and that Hackett would now bring Heaven down to Earth. The Queen, hearing this, immediately executed Hackett and the Puritans fled for the Netherlands, and later the New World.)

At any rate, an intelligence agency of one sort or other existed in England since the 1500s. Hitherto done on an *ad hoc* intermittent basis, however, it didn't become "professionalized" and fully state-funded until the First World War.

Called "the second oldest profession" by many historians, espionage had an unsavory reputation as the purview of traitors and prostitutes. Such as Rahab in the Old Testament— a lady of the night who betrayed her own people to act as a spy for Joshua's forces, who later came in and sacked Jericho. Or Delilah, from *The Book of Judges*, who uses her feminine wiles to betray Samson in order to aid the invading Philistines.

Aristotle in Book V of "Politics" has a section on "How Tyrannies Are Maintained," in which he describes the Persian technique of using women as human intelligence. He writes, "Such were those women whom the Syracusians called potagogides. Hiero also used to send out listeners wherever there was any meeting or conversation; for the people dare not speak with freedom for fear of such persons."

The following are profiles of some women who gathered intelligence during World War One who may, or may not, challenge comparison with the historical *femme fatales* who came before them.

Jeanne Florentine Bourgeois

Jeanne Florentine Bourgeois, more famously known by her stage name Mistinguett, was one of the most celebrated French performers of the early 20th century. Renowned for her singing, dancing, and charismatic presence on stage, Mistinguett captivated audiences across Europe. Like many celebrities, she was approached by Allied spymasters to see if she would engage in espionage. Parenthetically, it might be noted that performers were routinely recruited to be operatives due to the fact that they were usually welcome in all circles and very few people suspected them of being there for purposes of surveillance.

Born on April 3, 1875, in Enghien-les-Bains, France, Jeanne Florentine Bourgeois rose from humble beginnings. Her mother was a seamstress and her father, who owned a mattress factory, died when Jeanne was still very young.

Hers would be a hardscrabble childhood marked by privation and penury. Constantly doing odd-jobs and running errands to earn money, she dreamed of an escape from an existence of limited horizons and an unpromising future.

A trapdoor seemed to present itself in the form of the stage. The idea of performing first occurred to her when a famous Parisian entertainer named Anna Thibaud moved into the suburb and Jeanne's mother did some interior decorating for her.

Star-struck, Jeanne initially tried to ingratiate herself with Thibaud to see if she might mentor her. She asked what she needed to learn to succeed on the stage. Whereupon the seasoned actress responded, "To succeed in the theatre . . . you must be pretty. You must excite men."

Confused as to how she might excite an audience, Thibaud corrected her: "No, the men!"

To this Jeanne showed perplexity, at which point the veteran entertainer told her that she was too unattractive, anyway, and shouldn't even try.

The skinny girl, with too-big teeth, bristled and decided then and there to start taking singing lessons. It was then that she assumed her first stage name, "Princesse de la Pointe-Raquet".

When not busy taking classes, she would sell flowers on street corners and attract customers by singing in the Jardin des Tuileries or the Place de la Concorde. She would try to get little engagements in bistros or cafes. At the Eldorado, she would occasionally see her favorite performer, Alice Ozy.

Ozy was one of the most captivating and controversial figures of 19th-century Paris. Renowned for her beauty, charisma, and talent, she became a celebrated actress and courtesan during a time when the lines between the stage and society were often blurred. Like Jeanne, she was born into modest circumstances in Paris. From a young age, she demonstrated a flair for performance, and it wasn't long before she found her way to the stage. She began her career in the

Parisian theaters, where her beauty and talent quickly drew attention. Ozy's presence on stage was magnetic; she had an innate ability to captivate audiences with her dramatic flair and sensuality, which made her a favorite in the burgeoning theater scene of Paris.

During this period, Paris was undergoing significant social and cultural changes. The city was becoming the epicenter of the arts, with theaters and salons serving as key venues for social interaction and entertainment. In this vibrant environment, Ozy thrived, becoming a symbol of the allure and decadence that characterized the French Second Empire.

In addition to her career on the stage, Ozy became one of the most famous courtesans of her time. The role of a courtesan in 19th-century Paris was complex; these women were not just mistresses but often held significant influence over the men they associated with, many of whom were powerful figures in politics, art, and society. Ozy was no exception. She was known for her relationships with several high-profile men, including prominent politicians, artists, and writers.

One of her most notable relationships was with Prince Jérôme Napoléon, the nephew of Emperor Napoleon III. Their liaison was the subject of much gossip and intrigue, reflecting the close ties between the worlds of politics and entertainment in Paris. Ozy's ability to navigate these relationships with tact and intelligence further enhanced her status as a celebrity.

It was a boon to young Jeanne when Ozy took her under her wing and began teaching her the techniques of allurement: how to move, how to strike poses, how to hold a crowd's attention with provocative performances.

But more than just offering suggestions about tradecraft, Ozy introduced her to her manager, Monsieur Saint-Marcel, director of the revue at the Casino de Paris. It was he who gave Jeanne the stage name of "Miss Helyett." She worked for him for a while under this pseudonym until 1893 when he brought her under contract and changed her name again—this time to Mistinguett.

As her talents and reputation grew so did her legions of admirers, among whom were counted King Edward VII and Oscar Wilde.

Unfortunately, she also had less illustrious confederates. Principal among these was a man for whom she developed serious feelings. His name was Louis Leplée. A drug dealer and male prostitute, he introduced her to the seedier side of Montmartre with its sex shops and red light district.

He instigated a break between Jeanne and Saint-Marcel. It was sometime after that that she recovered her balance, broke with Leplée and staged a comeback.

Seeing the crowds she was drawing with her increasingly risqué performances, her new manager doubled her salary. Her legs were eventually insured for 500,000 francs.

It was about this time that she met a wealthy Brazilian suitor. They never married. Despite this fact he sired a child with her, named Léopold.

She continued to work up until she was six months' pregnant. Not a maternal woman, she sent Léopold to Brazil to be raised by his father down there.

Even though her personal life was in a shambles, her professional life continued to thrive. She was working better clubs and captivating a better calibre of suitor.

To everyone's shock, however, she ended up in a romantic entanglement with a man thirteen years her junior, named Maurice Chevalier.

She helped launch his career, insisting that if he were not cast in productions beside her she would not sign the contract.

She was enamored of the dashing Chevalier (as millions of other women would be in subsequent decades as his provincial celebrity flowered into international stardom).

But in those early years, he belonged only to Mistinguett.

Her suffering can be imagined when in August 1914, Chevalier was drafted. It was during this time that she began doing charity concerts to aid the war effort.

Her career as an intelligence asset began at about this time.

It was then that a colonel tried to enlist her help to infiltrate political circles and gather information. Disinclined to play the part of spy, the colonel pulled his trump card and told her that there was a certain captive in a prison camp in Spain. His name was Maurice Chevalier.

Beside herself with panic and anguish, she reluctantly agreed to act in the capacity of an intelligence operative. If she did so, she was assured, the French government would bring all its influence to bear to have Chevalier released.

She was issued false papers and given a German chauffeur (whose own family was being held hostage in order to extort his compliance). His job was to drive her to parties with influential people who were targeted for surveillance and to ensure that nothing happened to her.

The stress of pulling double duty as both an entertainer and a spy was perhaps too much for her. Because, eventually, she disobeyed orders and tried to break Chevalier out of the prisoner-of-war camp herself. The effort failed and Mistinguett was apprehended by the German military.

They attempted to get her to spy for *them*. She now faced the prospect of becoming a double agent. Given the fact that she didn't want to be a spy for one country, she shrank away from the prospect of playing an even more dangerous game. So she alerted her handlers back in France as to what was being floated. The Germans caught wind of the betrayal and immediately arrested her.

Slated to be executed, she was reprieved at the last moment when the French government swapped her out with the families of German nationals who had previously been interned in French camps.

Not long after she gained her freedom, she found out that negotiations had been made for Chevalier to be released as well.

Chevalier was less traumatized by his captivity than he was by the fact that, after returning to Paris, he felt as if he had been forgotten by the fickle crowds. Mistinguett once again used her influence and connections to kickstart his comeback.

Unfortunately, Chevalier soon threw over the older woman for a younger performer named Léonie Bathiat, known professionally as Arletty.

Mistinguett was devastated. She would later write that she considered Chevalier the love of her life. Her only consolation was that, later on (in World War Two), long after Arletty had broken up with Chevalier, she had taken up with a German officer and betrayed her country.

Arletty was arrested and tried for treason as a collaborator.

Decades later when fielding questions about the wisdom of taking up with a *Luftwaffe* officer, Arletty offered the vulgar excuse, *"Si mon coeur est français, mon cul, lui, est international."*

As for Mistinguett, she returned to her career in entertainment after the war, where she continued to captivate audiences well into the 1920s and 1930s. Her wartime activities remained largely unknown to the public during her lifetime, as she chose not to highlight this aspect of her life. Instead, she focused on her career and her enduring love for the stage.

Mistinguett's contributions to the war effort, however, were not forgotten by those who were aware of her work as a spy. She was recognized for her bravery and her willingness to risk her life, adding a layer of complexity to her public persona. Mistinguett was more than just a performer; she was a patriot who played a vital role in the defense of France during one of the darkest periods in its history.

Gabrielle Petit

Gabrielle Alina Eugenia Maria Petit was born on February 20, 1893, in the city of Tornai, in the Wallonia region of Belgium.

Her country, which was small but strategically-located, experienced significant economic growth and transformation in the years leading up to World War I. As one of the most industrialized nations in Europe at the time, Belgium's economy was characterized by a blend of traditional industries, such as textiles and agriculture, and rapidly expanding sectors like chemical processing, and railways. The coal-rich region of Wallonia, in particular, became the center of heavy industries such as steel production and machinery manufacturing.

Despite all the economic activity in her native Wallonia,

Gabrielle Petit scarcely had a share in what was otherwise a flourishing economy. Her father, Jules, called himself an engineer, though he was really a failed inventor, who frittered away his meager earnings on various get-rich-quick schemes. Due to his impracticality, his wife (Aline) had to carry most of the economic burden of the family, by giving piano lessons to local children.

The Petits were plunged into destitution when on July 6, 1902, Aline died after complications of heart surgery. She was only thirty-two years old. Her daughter, Gabrielle, was just nine.

Panicked and incapable of supporting his children, Jules placed his daughter Gabrielle and her older sister Hélène in an orphanage just three months after he was widowed.

Inmates in the orphanage of the Sisters of the Child Jesus in Brugelette, the two girls mopped floors, scrubbed tiles, peeled potatoes and were assigned to laundry detail. Their father scarcely visited them.

While Hélène adjusted herself to her new life as a *de facto* orphan, Gabrielle struggled. Having learned to be independent as a little girl due to the joint pressures of penury and neglect, she chafed under the new constraints imposed on her and tended to flout rules. Disillusionment born from her experiences with her father, she distrusted authority figures. This naturally bled over into her interactions with the women running the orphanage, who didn't appreciate the child's persistent impertinence.

The only time she settled in and felt at home is when she was tasked with being an assistant to one of the teachers. She enjoyed this job, and aspired to be an educator one day herself.

Her dreams were dashed, however, when she was eventually expelled in August of 1908 for unruly behavior.

The directress said, "Among the students, the pressure of someone who would have provoked authority could not be countenanced."

Of course, as subsequent social science experiments (like the Milgram Experiment in 1968) demonstrated, the most ethical type of person was the self-described curmudgeon, the trouble-maker, the gadfly to authority figures. Of all the subjects in Stanley Milgram's famous experiment, this personality-type was the only one who could not be coerced to torture others.

Gabrielle, as events would demonstrate, would conform to this stereotype of obduracy and ethical behavior. It would one day lead to a bronze statue of her likeness being placed in the Saint-Jean Square in Brussels. Few people casting glances at the upraised chin and noble aspect of that memorial would be able to appreciate just what a contrast her early life struck with posthumous glory.

For one thing, after being kicked out of the orphanage, she ran through a series of dead-end jobs and was even sporadically homeless.

At one point, in her early twenties, she provoked a scandal by moving in with a divorced man. After that relationship fizzled, she was once again on the streets. Luckily, she was taken in by Marie Collet, an old widow. The older woman helped her get on her feet. For a time, Gabrielle worked as a nanny. Then, after that, as a shopgirl in a store that sold furs.

It was during this period that she met Maurice Gobert. Though the two hit it off, there was a certain measure of volatility introduced into the relationship by Gobert's family, who distrusted Gabrielle "since she didn't come from a good family" . . . or any family at all, as it so happened.

Gobert's sister, in particular, tried to sabotage the couple's happiness.

Their relationship's tempestuous nature seemed to mirror the larger geopolitical turbulence of their country as Belgium tried to navigate the complexities of maintaining a neutral position in a continent rife with political tensions.

When war erupted in 1914, Belgium's diplomatic maneuvers ended in disappointment. Germany, under the Schlieffen Plan, sought to quickly defeat France by sweeping through Belgium, bypassing France's heavily fortified borders. The Schlieffen Plan called for German troops to march through Belgium, capturing its territory and outflanking French defenses. For Germany, Belgium's neutrality was little more than an obstacle to achieving its military objectives.

Germany presented an ultimatum to Belgium on August 2, 1914, demanding that it allow German forces to pass through its territory unopposed. Belgium, determined to uphold its neutrality and sovereignty, refused. This act of defiance placed Belgium in an unenviable position: on one side was the German Empire, a military behemoth prepared to use overwhelming force to achieve its goals; on the other side were France and Britain, both of whom expected Belgium to resist any German advances and maintain its neutral status.

Belgium's refusal to capitulate led to the German invasion on August 4, 1914. German forces quickly overran Belgian defenses, and the country was occupied for most of the war. Despite its small size and limited military resources, Belgium's resistance delayed the German advance, giving France and Britain valuable time to mobilize their forces. However, the price for Belgium was immense. Cities like Liège, Leuven, and Brussels were heavily bombarded, and the German occupation was marked by widespread destruction, civilian casualties, and atrocities, including the burning of libraries, churches, and historical buildings, as well as mass executions of civilians.

Like so many other young men Maurice Gobert enlisted in the military. He reportedly excelled in this new environment and was eventually made a non-commissioned officer.

He and Gabrielle planned to marry. But tragedy struck when a German attack left Gobert disabled. With both legs wounded, he was for a time confined to a wheelchair. Even more traumatizing to the youth was the fact that, in the chaos, he had been cut off from his regiment.

He desperately wanted to reunite with his troops. To do

that, however, he would have to cross into neutral Netherlands, go to England and cross back over into France to the one strip of Belgium still held by Belgian troops. To make the daunting trip, he'd need Gabrielle's help.

Up until then, she had no idea of the many escape networks that existed in her country. (One was run by Edith Cavell, a British nurse who would be lionized after the war for her bravery.)

Unfortunately, Gabrielle and Maurice weren't just handicapped by an ignorance of these networks, but also by the fact that Germany created the first electrified border on the Dutch-Belgian front called the Wire of Death.

When Germany invaded Belgium in August 1914, it was essential for the Germans to control the flow of people and information in and out of the country. The Netherlands, which had declared neutrality during the war, shared a 450-kilometer border with Belgium, and this boundary quickly became a focal point for those trying to escape the harsh realities of war. Thousands of Belgians, including civilians fleeing occupation, resistance fighters, spies, and Allied soldiers, used the porous border to escape into the Netherlands, hoping to reach safety or find passage to other countries.

Additionally, Belgium was a key battleground, and both sides of the conflict were eager to exploit the border for smuggling weapons, intelligence, and other supplies. The Germans, determined to stop these flows and tighten their grip on occupied Belgium, decided to construct a high-voltage electrified fence along the entire Dutch-Belgian border. This would effectively seal off Belgium from the Netherlands, cutting off escape routes and isolating Belgium further.

The Wire of Death was a formidable and terrifying structure. It stretched for about 200 kilometers (124 miles) along the border, from the North Sea coast to the German border in the east. The fence consisted of several layers of high-voltage electric wires, charged with 2,000 to 3,000 volts, which were more than enough to instantly kill anyone who made contact with them.

The structure typically stood three meters high and was supported by wooden poles. It was heavily guarded by German troops and supplemented with barbed wire, watchtowers, and regular patrols. In some sections, the fence was even buried underground to prevent people from digging tunnels beneath it.

While the fence was intended primarily as a deterrent to prevent people from crossing into the Netherlands, its lethal nature made it a symbol of terror for those living near the border. The German authorities also imposed severe punishments on those caught trying to cross the wire, making the attempt even more dangerous.

The Wire of Death had a devastating impact on the Belgian population. Thousands of people had already fled into the Netherlands by the time the fence was completed, but for those who remained, it represented a near-total physical and psychological barrier. Families were divided, and Belgian resistance fighters found their activities hampered by the fence. Many desperate people attempted to cross it despite the dangers, either to reunite with loved ones or to escape German occupation.

The human toll of the fence was significant. Although it is difficult to know the exact number, estimates suggest that between 1,000 and 3,000 people died trying to cross the Wire of Death. Many were electrocuted as soon as they touched the wire, while others were shot by German guards. Those who survived found ingenious ways to evade the deadly fence. Some created insulated gloves and boots, or used long wooden poles to try and lift the wires. Others paid local guides or smugglers to help them cross the border. A few even managed to bribe German soldiers to let them pass.

In addition to these escape attempts, the Wire of Death became a symbol of resistance. Some Belgian and Dutch citizens cut small holes in the fence to allow individuals to pass through, while others created underground networks to smuggle people across.

In the months that Gabrielle studied the situation and made sufficient contacts to help Maurice, their relationship ended. But not before she successfully arranged for him to be smuggled across the border.

His unflagging patriotism was not to be unmatched by Gabrielle's, who wanted to do her part by becoming a nurse to help the Belgian army. To join them, however, she (like Maurice) would have to make it to neutral Holland, and from there take a boat to England.

Once on the boat, she was recruited to be a spy. A man with whom she's struck up an idle conversation turned out to be in the British Secret Services. He invited her to London headquarters and her training in espionage began.

After a sufficient period of instruction, she was sent back to occupied Belgian to spy on the Germany Army in Western Hainaut.

She conducted her activities under the nom-de-guerre Mademoiselle LeGrande. It was while she was under this identity that she got a hotel room near the railroad tracks. From her vantage-point, she meticulously documented German supply chain arrivals and departures, as well as troop movements.

The most dangerous part of the work was sending her reports back to her handlers through the German Wire of Death. Couriers were notoriously unreliable. Moreover, the German military was getting better and better at getting moles into the spy network, who would report on intelligence operatives. As the economy collapsed and war placed its constraints on the population, a growing number of Belgians were happy to accept money from the Germans to inform on their own citizens.

Many moles posed as couriers.

Problems came to a head when Gabrielle's usual courier got arrested by German Intelligence and was replaced by a Dutch mole who fingered Gabrielle.

She was arrested on February 2, 1916. Incarcerated at the prison de Saint-Gilles, she was placed in solitary confinement for a month. Thinking that this would soften her up, her captors were bitterly disappointed when she refused to inform on any of the people she knew. Rather than submit to intimidation, Gabrielle's native temperament flared up and she was just as impertinent to the German case-officers as she had earlier been to the sisters at the orphanage.

Her custodians offered her amnesty in return for her cooperation. Instead what they got was Gabrielle shouting "Long live the king! Long live the king!"

She was returned to her cell.

At around this time, another girl who was Gabrielle's age (twenty-three) was arrested on similar charges. Her name was Germain Scaron. She was the daughter of a Belgian magistrate. She was a friend and confidante of Petit. Because Gabrielle refused to testify against her, the Germans released her for lack of evidence.

But back to her cell Gabrielle went, where she scrawled on the wall, "I want to show them that I don't give a damn!"

Meanwhile several other female spies had been brought in, each being released in turn after they made deals with the German occupiers.

Gabrielle alone remained.

The officer in charge was growing more desperate, knowing that if she didn't crack soon, orders would be handed down to execute her. And he was right. Despite pleading with her one last time to cooperate, Gabrielle refused to be cowed, instead saying, "I will show you how a Belgian woman faces death."

On April 1, 1916, she was killed by a firing squad.

Her brave response to danger galvanized Belgian resistance, and after the war she was held up as an example of patriotism, grit and determination. History remembers Gabrielle Petit not just for her feisty opposition to arbitrary authority, but for the moral example she set for future generations.

Despina Storch

Known as "The Turkish Delight" and "The Modern Cleopatra," Despina Storch ran a spy network whose block-chain comprised Berlin, Paris, London, Madrid, Rome and New York City. Internationalism came naturally to the exotic young woman, whose father was Bulgarian and whose mother was German. She herself was born in cosmopolitan Istanbul on January 1, 1895.

At the turn of the 20th century, the Ottoman Empire, though often described as the "Sick Man of Europe," remained a vast and diverse realm. Stretching across three continents, the empire was home to a mosaic of ethnicities, languages, and religions, contributing to a distinctive form of cultural heterogeneity. It was the perfect incubator for a future spy, who could pass easily from language to language, or pick up on the sensitive nuances of different habits, manners and mores.

At seventeen, Despina (born Despina Davidovitch) married a Frenchman named Paul Storch. The union soon ended in divorce—a circumstance that would later make her ex-husband uncomfortable as he was in the French army and his former-wife was spying on behalf of its enemies.

In Paris, she was known as Madame Nezie; in Madrid and London, she was Madame Hesketh; in Rome, he was Madame Davidovitch; in New York, Madame Despina; and in Washington, DC, she was known as Baroness de Bellville.

Her spying career lasted for seven years, and pre-dated the war.

Two weeks before hostilities broke out, she was already tasked by German Intelligence to penetrate into Russian aristocratic circles to gather information about sensitive military operations. There she befriended the handsome prince Sergius Soubnekoff, scion to one of Russia's most wealthy and well-connected families. Before Despina had arrived on the scene, Soubenkoff had already caused a scandal by falling in love with a commoner (a ballet dancer), with whom he eloped.

The aristocracy looked down their noses at the *mésalliance.* Nevertheless, the prince ignored his detractors and took a leave of absence from his regiment to go on a honeymoon with his new bride to Paris and Madrid. When he was called back to Russia by his commander, he left his wife back in Western Europe, where she was befriended by Despina Storch. The two attended parties together and, slowly, after gaining her confidence, the latter was able to pump the unwitting ballerina for information about her husband and his military activities.

After World War One began and Germany went to war against Russia, Soubenkoff was frustrated after his regiment had been mown down. He concluded that someone had to be tipping off German High Command as to Russian troop movements. Eventually, he initiated an investigation that uncovered the fact that Despina Storch had not just used his wife to gain entry to St. Petersburg's loftiest social circles, but that she had seduced a certain Colonel Miasoyedoff, who had been induced to share sensitive information. The investigation also uncovered that the minister of war was also betraying secrets. He ended up imprisoned for life, whereas Miasoyedoff was hanged.

As for Despina Storch?

By the time Soubenkoff caught wind of her activities, she had already left for Zurich, Switzerland.

German Intelligence later assigned her to Paris, London, Madrid and the Italian Riviera, where she attended parties, attracted admirers and sent reports back to the General Staff in Berlin. Most of her work was used as leverage against those whom she compromised.

In Madrid, she was seen going about with her companion, the Baron de Beville (later corrupted to "de Bellville"). The couple were sought for questioning when French authorities complained to Spanish counterparts that she had stolen valuable French military documents which she planned to pass on to the Germans. (The plans involved a French policy change whereby they were going to increase the duration of compulsory service from two years to three. The German Intelligence Service knew this even before it was announced in France. The investigators looking into the leak blamed Storch, who had gotten the information from an infatuated admirer, after which she passed it on to Herr Max Steinhauer, chief of the German Intelligence Bureau.)

Despina narrowly escaped arrest and deportation from Spain when a wealthy banker in Madrid named José Pascuale intervened on her behalf and used his pull in government to get Storch and de Beville released. She was warned to leave Spain within forty-eight hours. It was later revealed that Pascuale was also working for German Intelligence. He, too, later fled Spain.

As for Despina, she was soon seen in London. Dressed in black attire, she was introduced at parties as Madame Hesketh, a recent widow. She claimed that her husband had been an Englishman whose regiment was in India, but who had been killed when his troops had been reassigned to fight the Turks in one of their Asian provinces.

There she set up shop by creating a fake charity, pretending to receive donations for British soldiers. In her guise as a war widow, she chatted with all those who wanted to leave donations. Little by little, she gathered pieces of information together from a disparate number of sources that allowed her to cobble together information about the expansion of the British campaign in Egypt and Palestine.

Her activities in England were complicated when her handler, Hans Lodi (one of Germany's most accomplished spies), was discovered. He had been running a sophisticated spy network, but his identity came out when another asset under his command (Berthe Trost) had her cover blown while she was running a shop on Bond Street.

As British Intelligence was trying to trace all the nodes in the network, Despina hopped a boat and veritably disappeared.

No one knew where she was for months, until she turned up in San Juan, Puerto Rico (then a hub for German Intelligence, who used it as a beachhead to spread propaganda into the United States). From there, she was soon seen in Washington, DC (under the name of Baroness de Bellville), after which she soon moved into lavish rooms at the Biltmore Hotel in New York. Paid $1,000 a week by German Intelligence, she spent it on a dazzling wardrobe and chauffeur-driven limousines.

At about this time, the Department of Justice began to show interest in her and her companion, the Baron. One of the wealthiest men in New York at the time, W.H. Vanderpoel, volunteered to help the DOJ capture her. After being briefed about her, he was instructed to attend certain parties of elite socialites until, one day, the Baron de Beville thought it an advantageous thing to introduce the young man to Despina.

Thinking that he would make a wonderful contact, she was delighted when he seemed to want to spend more time with her. While she assumed that he would help her identify prospective targets for her activities and introduce her to various powerful people, he was sending his reports back to the DOJ's Investigation Bureau.

The time for her apprehension came when she casually dropped a comment about the fact that she soon planned to leave for Havana, Cuba. Vanderpoel feigned despondency at her departure and asked if he could accompany her as far as Washington, DC, where she was to board a train for Key West (after which she planned to board a boat for the Caribbean). She consented. And when the young man said his final goodbyes, he nodded to a group of waiting men, who boarded the train along with Despina and de Beville.

In Key West, they told the couple that they couldn't board the boat to Havana due to having defective passports. They'd have to go back to Washington, DC to get new ones. It was there that they were arrested.

While in custody, the authorities learned from Vanderpoel that Despina had had a safety deposit box in New York City. During her incarceration, they gained access to the box and obtained a wealth of information. Their eyes widened as they discovered her secret code, her relation to other spies in the network (such as Madame Nix and Count de Claremont), as well as a cache of cablegrams, correspondence and sensitive documents. Soon Scotland Yard began to share information that they had had regarding her activities in Great Britain. France too began to coordinate with the Department of Justice to trace her movements on the Continent and to create an influence-map documenting the wider network.

All the while, Despina found herself hobnobbing with a coarser crowd in an Ellis Island penitentiary. It was there that she was informed that she would be deported back to France.

"To France!" she reportedly said. "That will be the end of everything! The sun will never shine for me again!"

According to the official account she soon took ill of pneumonia and died at the tender age of twenty-three. Many historians point out, however, that her symptoms bore more resemblance to cyanide poisoning. As to whether she had had a secret cyanide capsule hidden somewhere on her person or not will have to remain an enduring mystery. But among the facts that we do know, she made one final daring escape—this time from the Physical Plane to the Great Hereafter on March 30, 1918.

Louise de Bettignies

Born on July 5, 1880, Louise de Bettignies ran one of the largest spy networks in World War One, called the Alice Network. (Her *nom-de-guerre* was Alice Dubois.) She was from a once-prosperous family that derived originally from Mons, in what is now Belgium. Her ancestors created porcelain in Tournai (where another spy, Gabrielle Petit, was from).

By the twentieth century, however, the House of Bettignies had lost most of its money and status. Nevertheless, Louise's father made sure to give his daughter an excellent education. She spoke English, German and Italian (as well as understanding Spanish, Czech and Russian). At eighteen, she went to England to study at Oxford. She moved back to France and finished her education at the University of Lille.

After this, she landed a job as a governess and tutor. She was initially employed by the wealthy Visconti family in Italy, then to Princess Elvira of Bavaria. Eventually, she was offered a job, tutoring the crown-prince of Austria, Ferdinand Joseph. But she had to decline this opportunity, as she contracted appendicitis and had to move back to live with her family in France.

Like so many others, her life was upended by World War One. Even after she recovered, her country did not. When Germany laid siege to Lille, Louise offered her assistance at hospitals and brought food and weapons to soldiers. It was then that she decided to fight back in her own way, via espionage. Thus was born her alter-ego, Alice Dubois.

Her second life began as a result of the refugee-crisis the war had caused, as people fled Belgium and the Netherlands. Worried about the German spies who would be infiltrating these masses of fleeing people, the British set up a vetting process. Military personnel would interview purported refugees trying to get into England. This had a dual purpose: firstly, it might help identify intelligence agents from Berlin peppered throughout the crowds; and, secondly, it aided the

British in their efforts to gather information from real refugees about German-occupied areas.

The problem with this process was that it was slow. As a result, Louise (aka Alice) fretted about information she had obtained from a family whose house had been occupied by a German officer. From them, she had learned about a plan whereby the Germans intended to dig tunnels under Allied trenches with the intention of wiring them with explosives. Though she had sent word ahead to the British to warn them, she had little faith that the intelligence would be passed on to the right channels in time to avoid disaster. As a result, she boarded a boat to sail to England to make certain that someone there knew about the plot.

By the time she arrived in the port town of Folkstone, she was greeted by representatives from British Intelligence's MI-6 unit and told, "Madame, before your foot touches the ground, please accept the congratulations and the thanks of the British army that you have saved."

So they *had* received the information!

Impressed by her linguistic skills and pluck, they were even more awed by her ingenuity. For instance, when people wanted to get messages out of occupied France, Louise transcribed their letters to a garment, re-writing the words in invisible lemon juice on a petticoat. Once in Allied territory, she would iron the fabric, which darkened the writing (revealing the messages) and cut the petticoat in sections, whereupon she mailed the pieces to their respective recipients.

There were so many people trying to get messages out to relatives that they called this courier service "the family post".

Both the British and the French vied to engage Louise's services. In the end, practicality won out, because, due to France being occupied, she couldn't hope to receive payment for her efforts until after the war. The British, by contrast, could remunerate her immediately. So she opted to enter the employ of Britain's MI-6.

It was in Folkstone that she received her formal instruction in the arts of espionage from a certain Major Lord Cameron (the same man who trained Gabrielle Petit). His code-name was "Uncle Edward".

Agents under Cameron's guidance were trained to observe and report on German troop movements, transport routes, and supply depots without attracting suspicion. This involved using everyday items like letters or clothing to conceal messages and intelligence.

Cameron also trained his pupils in the use of effective counterintelligence, stressing the importance of secrecy and how to avoid detection by the enemy. This involved using code names, secure methods of communication, and tactics for misleading German counterintelligence efforts.

Network-building was also of critical importance. Espionage, after all, was not a solo operation; it required the ability to recruit and manage local informants and couriers. Cameron's agents, like de Bettignies, were responsible for running entire networks of spies, and his training emphasized the importance of delegation, organization, and trust.

Lastly, his students were trained in methods for survival under pressure, including how to maintain a cover story and withstand interrogation.

As for Louise . . .

Once her education drew to a successful conclusion, she was sent back to the Continent (clad in another petticoat with invisible letters written in response to the ones she had initially brought).

She set to work immediately, building up the infrastructure of the new network that she was tasked with running. Eventually, it consisted of more than 80 agents who provided crucial intelligence to the British military. These agents operated within forty kilometers of the front to the west and east of Lille, gathering information on German troop movements, supply lines, and military installations. De Bettignies herself was responsible for coordinating their efforts, receiving reports, and passing the information to British Intelligence. She was so adept at her work that her superiors in England called her "the queen of spies".

And it wasn't just her superiors whom she inspired with confidence. Those who worked under her in the network felt the same way. An operative named Victor Viaene, whom she recruited, said, "One just had to follow her; it seemed impossible to refuse."

Another operative, Marie-Léonie Vanhoutte, said, "I was ready to follow her anywhere, for I knew instinctively that she was a girl capable of great things."

Louise divided her territory into sectors to identify German ammunition stores, co-opting ambulances to act as de facto courier vehicles that could move freely between sensitive areas, as well as recording German troop movements.

One operative working under her was a certain Madame Levengle, who lived near a train station. The Germans, of course, discouraged anyone who seemed to loiter in the area or seemed to be taking notes. Madame Levengle had the advantage of living right across from the train station. From an upper window, she watched the comings and goings of train shipments and observed how many cars contained German soldiers. To anyone who casually glanced up at the window, it would appear that she was knitting in a rocking chair.

All the while, however, she would tap her feet on the floor to signal to her two children on the storey below to record the numbers that she was telegraphing to them with the raps. To all outward observers, though, it merely looked like the children were doing their homework.

This situation was all the more remarkable because she had had part of her home commandeered by the German rail marshal, who had no idea what was going on.

Madame Levengle would pass on her reports to de Bettignies, who would encrypt the information and pass it on to British Intelligence.

Her network included many such men and women, from all walks of life, who worked as communications specialists, chemists, and saboteurs. Many of these operatives were civilians living in occupied territories, making them less likely to arouse German suspicion. Some worked as railway employees, civil servants, or in other roles where they could observe and report on German activities without drawing undue attention to themselves.

The Alice Network operated using a variety of covert techniques. Messages were often concealed in ordinary objects such as loaves of bread, articles of clothing, or catalogues for dry-goods companies. Many of the agents lived at crossroads, where surveillance of troop movements could be undertaken, and de Bettignies trained her agents in how to avoid detection and evade capture. The network's ability to blend into the civilian population and the use of creative methods of communication made it highly effective in gathering information without raising alarms.

The information gathered by the Alice Network had a profound impact on the war effort, particularly in northern France. One of the most significant contributions made by the network was its role in providing advance warning of German troop build-ups before the commencement of the Battle of Verdun, allowing the French and British armies to prepare their defenses and avoid disastrous losses.

Louise de Bettignies was eventually arrested by German authorities in 1915. This took place after the capture of her second-in-command, the aforementioned Marie-Léonie Vanhoutte. Under interrogation, the Germans tricked the younger woman into accidentally identifying de Bettignies from a series of photographs. Once this was done, they dispatched officials to arrest her.

After her capture, de Bettignies was sentenced to death, though her sentence was later commuted to forced labor. She died in captivity in 1918 due to illness. Despite this, her efforts left a lasting legacy in the history of espionage, and she was posthumously honored by both France and Britain for her bravery.

Sarah Aaronsohn

Born in 1890 in Zikhron Ya'akov, a small agricultural village in Ottoman-controlled Palestine, Sarah Aaronsohn was raised in a devout Jewish family that had emigrated from Romania. Her parents, Efraim and Malkah, were part of the First Aliyah, an early wave of Jewish immigration to Palestine in the late 19th century. Sarah was the youngest of six siblings, one of whom—Aaron Aaronsohn—would later become a world-renowned agronomist and a pivotal figure in her story.

The Aaronsohn family was highly educated and deeply connected to the nascent Zionist movement, which sought to establish a Jewish homeland in Palestine. Their upbringing was steeped in both Jewish tradition and a forward-thinking approach to science, agriculture, and politics. Sarah herself was an intelligent and assertive woman, characteristics that set her apart from many of her contemporaries in an era when women were largely relegated to domestic roles.

The outbreak of World War I in 1914 had profound consequences for the Middle East. The Ottoman Empire, which had controlled Palestine for centuries, entered the war on the side of the Central Powers (Germany and Austria-Hungary), pitting them against the Allied Powers, including Britain and France. Life under Ottoman rule became increasingly harsh, especially for the Jewish community, which suffered from food shortages, oppressive taxation, and the threat of conscription into the Ottoman army.

The Aaronsohn family, like many other Jews in Palestine, initially found themselves in a precarious position. While some Jews supported the Ottomans, others, including Sarah and her brother Aaron, believed that the British Empire was the better ally for the Zionist cause. The British had already shown some sympathy toward the idea of a Jewish homeland, and the Aaronsohns hoped that a British victory in the Middle East would lead to the establishment of a Jewish state.

As the war dragged on, Aaron Aaronsohn, who had been traveling extensively in Europe and America due to his work in agronomy, became increasingly convinced that the Ottoman Empire was doomed to collapse. He also recognized the strategic importance of providing the British with intelligence about Ottoman troop movements and military plans in Palestine and the surrounding region. It was from this realization that the idea for a Jewish spy network—later named NILI—was born. (It was from a Hebrew acronym, *Netzach Yisrael Lo Yeshaker*, which means "The Eternal One of Israel Will Not Lie".)

Aaron, along with his sister Sarah and several other close associates, including Avshalom Feinberg and Naaman Belkind, began to organize the NILI network in 1915. Their goal was to provide the British with detailed information about the Ottoman forces in Palestine, thus aiding the British war effort and increasing the chances of a British victory in the region. In exchange, they hoped that the British would support the establishment of a Jewish state after the war.

Sarah Aaronsohn's involvement in the NILI network was pivotal. After spending several months traveling through Ottoman-controlled territory, during which she witnessed firsthand the brutality of the regime, including the Armenian Genocide, she returned to Zikhron Ya'akov deeply disturbed by what she had seen. The atrocities she witnessed during her travels strengthened her resolve to work against the Ottoman Empire, and she soon became one of the key figures in the NILI network.

Unlike many other women of her time, Sarah was not content with playing a secondary role in the war effort. She was actively involved in gathering and transmitting intelligence to the British, often taking significant risks to ensure the success of the network. Her role included coding and decoding messages, coordinating with British agents via carrier pigeons, and even acting as a courier on occasion. She quickly became the de facto leader of NILI when her brother Aaron was abroad.

Sarah's efforts were not only motivated by a desire to see the Ottoman Empire defeated but also by her deep commitment to the Zionist cause. She believed that by helping the British, she was advancing the dream of a Jewish homeland. In her letters, she often expressed her belief that the Jewish people had a duty to actively fight for their future, rather than passively waiting for salvation.

The activities of the NILI network were extremely dangerous. The Ottomans had a strong intelligence apparatus in place, and anyone caught spying for the enemy could expect to be executed. Moreover, NILI's operations were complicated by the fact that they were based in Palestine, a region with a relatively small population and a tightly controlled Ottoman administration. Any unusual activity could easily arouse suspicion.

Sarah and her fellow NILI members had to constantly evade detection, using secret codes, ciphers, and covert methods of communication to transmit information to the British. They operated in a world where a single mistake could mean death, not only for themselves but also for their families and friends.

Despite these challenges, NILI succeeded in providing the British with crucial intelligence throughout the war. Their information helped the British army plan its Palestine Campaign, including General Edmund Allenby's decisive victory at the Battle of Beersheba in 1917. NILI's contributions were highly valued by British intelligence, and their work was considered instrumental in the eventual British victory in the Middle East.

In September 1917, NILI's luck ran out. The Ottoman authorities, who had long been suspicious of the activities of the Aaronsohn family and their associates, finally intercepted one of NILI's carrier pigeons carrying a coded message to the British. The Ottomans were able to crack the code and quickly realized that they had uncovered a sophisticated spy network operating right under their noses.

On October 1, 1917, Ottoman forces descended on Zikhron Ya'akov, arresting several members of the Aaronsohn family and other NILI operatives. Sarah Aaronsohn, realizing that the network had been compromised, took a drastic step to protect her comrades. Rather than flee, she chose to stay behind and destroy as much evidence as possible, knowing that this would likely lead to her capture.

When Sarah was eventually arrested, she endured several days of brutal interrogation and torture at the hands of the Ottoman authorities. Despite the physical and psychological torment she suffered, she refused to reveal any information about NILI or its members. Her silence allowed several key figures in the network to escape capture, and her actions are remembered as a testament to her extraordinary courage and loyalty to her cause.

After four days of torture, Sarah Aaronsohn made a final, desperate decision. On October 9, 1917, she managed to smuggle a gun into her cell and attempted to take her own life. Although she survived the initial gunshot wound, she died several days later from her injuries, marking the end of her short but extraordinary life at the age of 27.

Sarah Aaronsohn's death was a devastating blow to the NILI network, but her legacy lived on. Her brother Aaron continued to work with British intelligence after the war, and NILI's contributions were formally recognized by the British government. The information that NILI had provided helped the British secure control of Palestine, which eventually led to the Balfour Declaration in November 1917—Britain's public support for the establishment of a "national home for the Jewish people" in Palestine.

Sarah Aaronsohn's role in this pivotal moment in history, though often overlooked, was significant. Her courage, intelligence, and dedication to the Zionist cause made her one of the most remarkable figures in the history of World War I espionage. Today, she is remembered as a heroine of the Jewish people and a symbol of the sacrifices made in the fight for a Jewish homeland.

Chapter Four

From female operatives of intelligence agencies we move on to the topic of women who worked as war correspondents (the press being a sort of "intelligence agency for the people"). Instead of reporting back to spymasters, these women reported back to their editors.

As early as the Spanish-American War, the United States, for one, used female journalists to cover the events. Leading up to that watershed, there had been numerous journalists like Nelly Bly, who captured the public's imagination with her death-defying reporting, such as getting herself locked up in a mental asylum to tell the public about the conditions therein, or riding aloft the clouds in a hot-air balloon to replicate Jules Verne's novel "Around the World in Eighty Days". Such "stunt-reporting" turned women from journalists into celebrities. When World War One happened, George Lorimer of the *Saturday Evening Post* saw the value in assigning female writers to cover the conflict.

His actions were less shaped by a sympathy for feminism than by shrewd business sense. As public relations expert Edward Bernays said in his 1928 book "Propaganda," if one wants to sell a new product or idea, imagine that the crowd one is addressing is female. Women, after all, accounted for upwards of ninety percent of household purchases, he explained.

George Lorimer understood this principle. For him, the more women readers he had, the more advertisers he could attract to his magazine.

In the age of the "New Woman," as it was called, and "Thoroughly Modern Millie," he saw value in getting leading female novelists and writers (such as Edith Wharton or Mary Roberts Rinehart) to act as war correspondents. In fact, there was much griping from male journalists that the latter (Mary Roberts Rinehart) scooped them in being the first person to write about the new trench warfare.

And it wasn't just the *Saturday Evening Post* that saw the value in female war correspondents. *Good Housekeeping, Woman's Home Companion, The Delineator, Pictorial Review, the Ladies Home Journal*, and many other publications sent female journalists to cover the war.

In the foregoing chapter, a passing reference was made to the Armenian Genocide at the hands of the Ottoman Empire. In the upcoming pages, we will gain a bird's-eye view of the event in question from a journalist named Eleanor Franklin Egan (1879 – 1925), who witnessed the events firsthand.

From the February 6, 1916 edition of the *Saturday Evening Post*, we read:

Behind the great curtain of battle across the entrance to the Dardanelles and on Gallipoli Peninsula terrible things have been happening in Turkey these months past. When that curtain lifts, and not before, the full details will be revealed of one of the most astounding scenes in history. The Committee of Union and Progress of the Young Turk Government, who are of the Company of the House of Faith, which is Islam, are engaged in the congenial task of dispersing two million Christian Ottoman subjects—the Armenians.

However the performance may be referred to in the outside world, that is what the Turks call it—"dispersing". Quietly, systematically, with a fixed intent, the work goes on; and already a million and a half of the hated tribe have been driven from their homes, with an incidental loss of life among them estimated at above eight hundred thousand. An exaggeration? We must wait until the curtain lifts. These were the figures whispered to me in Constantinople, always with an assurance that they minimized rather than overstated the facts.

From the beginning Christian protest has not been wanting. The Sublime Porte has been repeatedly besieged by appeals and approached with carefully guarded warnings of a future settlement; but the Sublime Porte has been arrogant and immovable. Indeed, the Sublime Porte is impatient of outside interference these days and has answered warnings with threats.

In writing about this fearful thing one must, for obvious reasons, be cautious. Names and exact localities cannot be mentioned without fear of getting somebody into trouble. Everything that is written about Turkey and about Germany in Turkey gets back to Constantinople in some mysterious way almost as soon as it is published, and information bureaus are organized in minutest detail. Specific reference is not necessary anyhow; not yet. The scene of actual atrocities embraces all Asia Minor, and there is not a town with Armenians in it that has not long since felt the heavy hand of government.

The reports came from Constantinople slowly and by devious underground routes; and so ever present and breathless was the fear of retaliatory massacre in the city itself that nobody would speak freely, nobody would tell all he knew, and written communications were concealed or destroyed as though the possession of them constituted the highest crime. I brought out with me, and had with me through five days' detention on the border of Turkey, a copy of the original order that was posted in Armenian towns and communities throughout Asia Minor sometime in June.

A Copy of the Proclamation

I was told in London and am assured by Armenian societies here that mine is the first copy of this document to be brought out of Turkey. I find it difficult to believe this, but after making careful inquiry I have decided that it must be true. I do know that bringing it out was for me a dangerous venture. I mentioned it in my story of five days in a Turkish prison and have since had a number of inquiries as to how I managed to conceal it. One stranger friend in the West hazards the guess that I had it between the lining and the leather of my shoe. No, nothing so easily guessable. I had it copied on the innermost inner margins of a perfectly harmless-looking book which I was more or less ostentatiously reading when the Turkish examiner came aboard my train. He picked the book up, shook it, ran its pages with his thumb a few times, and subjected it to what he doubtless considered a careful scrutiny, but none of the hazardous penciling revealed themselves and I was permitted to carry it off to prison with me, while the wholly uncompromising notes which were taken away from me went back to Constantinople to be passed on by the censor there.

I don't mind admitting that during my five days' suspense under the eyes of an armed guard that book became to me an object of curious dread. And with reason too. My keepers were ignorant Turks whose instructions were not to permit anybody to carry a written line across the border; I had outwitted them for the moment, a thing no Turk can stand in any case, and if by chance they had discovered my suspicious looking and so carefully hidden notes the word "perilous" would not have been too melodramatic to use in describing my situation. I think I should probably have figured as the party of the first part in a mysterious disappearance. The proclamation reads:

"Our fellow countrymen, the Armenians, who form one of the racial elements of the Ottoman Empire, having taken up, as a result of foreign instigation for many years past, with a lot of false ideas of a nature to disturb the public order; and because of the fact that they have brought about bloody happenings and have attempted to destroy the peace and security of the Ottoman state, the safety and interests of their fellow countrymen, as well as of themselves; and, moreover, as they have now dared to join themselves to the enemy of their existence"—Russia—"and to the enemies now at war with our state—our government is compelled to adopt extraordinary measures and sacrifices, both for the preservation of the order and security of the country and for the welfare and the continuation of the existence of the Armenian society. Therefore, as a measure to be applied until the conclusion of the war, the Armenians have to be sent away to places which have been prepared in the interior vilayets; and a literal obedience to the following orders, in a categorical manner, is accordingly enjoined on all Ottomans:

"First—All Armenians, with the exception of the sick, are obliged to leave within five days from the date of this proclamation, by villages or quarters, and under the escort of the gendarmerie.

"Second—Though they are free to carry with them on their journey the articles of their movable property which they desire, they are forbidden to sell their lands and their extra effects, or to leave the latter here and there with other people, because their exile is only temporary and their landed property and the effects they will be unable to take with them will be taken care of under the supervision of the government, and stored in closed and protected buildings. Anyone who sells or attempts to take care of his movable effects or landed property in a manner contrary to this order shall be sent before the Court Martial. They are free to sell to the government only the articles which may answer the needs of the army.

"Third—Contains a promise of safe conduct.

"Fourth—A threat against anyone attempting to molest them on the way.

"Fifth—Since the Armenians are obliged to submit to this decision of the government, if some of them attempt to use arms against the soldiers or gendarmes, arms shall be employed against them and they shall be taken dead or alive. In like manner those who, in opposition to the government's decision, refrain from leaving or seek to hide themselves, if they are sheltered or given food and assistance, the persons who thus shelter or aid them shall be sent before the Court-Martial for execution."

The Revolt at Van

It is not difficult to picture the reign of terror that ensued through out Armenian Turkey and in all Armenian settlements on the post ing of this proclamation. It struck down the hands of two million Christian people and left them in a state of helplessness beyond words to describe. It did not leave them even the refuge of friendship; and the promises of protection, both as to life and to property, were not to be taken seriously, as everybody knew. It was a literal order for banishment and confiscation, and the only way any Armenian could escape it was by turning Mohammedan.

It has always been the Turkish habit to make whole Christian communities within Ottoman borders pay for the offenses of individual citizens or of small rebellious groups; but this fact does not quite explain the present unprecedented movement.

At the beginning of the war some Armenians on the border between Turkey and Russia—Armenians who had felt the weight of Turkish oppression always, and many of whose people had been victims of the massacres of Abdul-Hamid—went over and joined the Russian Army; while an organized body of them placed themselves in armed opposition to the Turkish forces at Van. This was unfortunate; and, since it was open rebellion, it called for the usual punishment, which no nation would deny Turkey the right to inflict. But the rebels represented but a handful of the great Armenian population, and the wholesale retaliation which has been meted out and is being meted out by the government now is so far beyond the bounds of necessity or reasonable excuse that it can be regarded only as another exhibition of the characteristic national shortsightedness and stupidity which have made so many pages of Turkey's modern history amazing to an intelligent world.

How the Armenians got arms nobody knows. It is and has been for many years a capital offense for any of them to carry weapons; but because there were arms along the eastern border it became expedient to assume that they were scattered throughout the country, and the methods of torture practiced on the luckless people to get them to reveal the hiding places of their mythical stores of guns and ammunition are too horrible to write about.

One man, an American doing business in Turkey, tells of getting off a train at a station not far from Constantinople and of seeing a man behaving in a most extraordinary manner. He was dancing along on his toes and shrieking with what sounded like maniacal laughter. The American asked a bystander what the trouble was with him and was told that he had just been undergoing bastinado. The bystander was a Turk and he delivered this information with a laugh.

Another man, an Armenian, in writing about the scenes of torture, says with a sort of plaintive simplicity: "In the old days anywhere from twenty-five to fifty strokes were considered enough, but now they don't stop under a hundred strokes and sometimes they give as many as two hundred. The calves of the legs swell and burst; the victim faints and is revived time and again, and many of them lose their reason under it."

Though the Armenian is a brave man if he has a fighting chance, aggressiveness in a political sense is conspicuously absent in the racial character. They are a people subdued by fear and desiring only to live in peace. If they had been capable of organized and general revolt against Turkish rule they would have risen long ago, if for no other purpose than to wreak vengeance on their age-long oppressors.

It is not fear of Armenian rebellion that is actuating the Young Turks now. It is the same jealousy, cupidity and fanatic racial hatred which, given free rein for longer than we know, has engendered in the very nature of the Turk a belief in his right to plunder and to persecute these people. The little rebellion on the far border of the country gave them a much-desired excuse for action at a time when all eyes are fixed on more far-reaching and important events; when great tragedies are dwarfed by greater tragedies and may be expected to strike soundlessly and resultless against the sensibilities of a tragedy-numbed world.

Everybody knows about the attempted launching of a Holy War when Turkey was drawn into this bewildering conflict. Throughout the Ottoman Empire the imams in the mosques read to the thronging, excited crowds the extraordinary declaration. It is a long and complicated address, but in every line it shrieks a fanatic hatred so far removed from what used to be twentieth-century concepts that it sounds like nothing but medieval madness.

"It is necessary to form secret and public unions in the land of Islam," it says. "It is necessary that the people should know from to-day that the Holy War has become a sacred duty, and that the blood of infidels in Islamic lands may be shed with impunity, except those to whom the Moslem power has given security and those who are confederate with it. . . .

"They must know that the killing of infidels has become a sacred duty, whether it be secretly or openly, as the great Koran declares in its word: 'Take them and kill them wherever you come across them, and we have given you a manifest power over them by revelation.'. . .

"To whoever kills one single infidel of those who rule over Islamic lands, either secretly or openly, there is a reward like a reward from all the living ones of the Islamic world. And let every individual of the Islamic world, in whatever place he may be, take upon him an oath to kill at least three or four of the infidel enemies of God and enemies of religion. He must take upon him this oath before God Most High, expecting his reward from God alone; and let the Moslem be confident, if there be to him no other good deed than this, nevertheless, he will prosper in the Day of Judgment."

This declaration of a Holy War had nothing to do with the Armenian horrors in Turkey; but it preceded those horrors just long enough to have roused Mohammedan fanaticism to a point where few Turks have any compunction in carrying out the hideous orders of the government.

The Turks knew and have openly declared that the proclamation calling for the removal of all Armenians to the interior was intended for nothing but to give a color of justice to the procedure and to cover secret instructions which were sent throughout the districts marked for immediate depopulation, instructions that withdrew from the Armenians all protection of law.

I have already said that a million and a half have been removed, with a reported mortality among them of more than eight hundred thousand. No details could add to the frightfulness of the picture these figures present, but details are not wanting. The process of removal is a simple one, since it involves no responsibility on the part of the government for the welfare of the exiles. Secret agents are sent into the towns and villages, with powers that give them command over all local authorities; they post the proclamation and, with the aid of carefully organized and well-rewarded espionage, see that it is literally obeyed. The pitiless sentence, "All Armenians must leave," does not mean that the government undertakes to gather them up and transport them to the places of exile. It means that they must report to a headquarters, learn where they are to go, either their final destination or a concentration camp, and then proceed on their own responsibility and entirely at their own expense. They must abandon their business, their affairs of all kinds, their homes, and everything they possess that they cannot carry with them in their hands or on their backs; and they must submit without a murmur to any indignities that may be heaped on them. It is said that when companies gather to start on the march, the Turks, their very neighbors, and especially Turkish women, crowd their trail like jackals and take away from them, without a chance of interference from the gendarmes, anything they may happen to want; so that many a helpless band goes off empty-handed, stripped of everything except such money and small treasures as they may happen to have concealed about them. And it was not to be expected that some of the Moslem populations—Turks, Kurds and Arabs—would long be content with the monotony of dispersal. They soon grew tired of it and resorted in many places to the old and established methods of wholesale butchery. From various points have come reports of massacres as deliberate and complete as those Abdul-Hamid organized and directed during the years from 1894 to 1897. Whole towns have been wiped out, and when I left Turkey there was a growing fear that the slower process would be abandoned for more expeditious measures throughout the empire. I might say here that it is generally believed that the Sultan, Mohammed V, is as strongly opposed to this performance as he is capable of being opposed to anything. Abdul-Hamid's massacres were his own, devised and ordered by himself; but his successor, who was his prisoner for thirty years, has milder and less cowardly views of things. He is not much in the way of a statesman or man of affairs. How could he be? He was only two years younger than his brother; he never had any real expectation of coming to the throne; and he was confined to his palace and about half a mile of territory round it during the entire time that Abdul-Hamid reigned.

Surrounded by spies and never permitted to see anybody or to know anything of the country's affairs, his favorite pastimes were playing the piano and drinking himself into a state of placid indifference. He plays the piano yet—very well, they say—and he has no taste for blood. He likes neither the war nor the massacres, and has uttered his feeble protest against both. This was told me by a man who knows the Sultan well, speaks his language, and has talked with him freely many times.

The Armenians are an industrious and prosperous element in the Ottoman population. They are the merchants, the bankers, the progressive students of modern life and methods, the teachers, the scientists. In humbler walks of life they are the capable and trusted servants, watchmen and guardians of property, while such advance in agriculture as has been made in Turkey is almost wholly due to their progressiveness and characteristic ambition. They accumulate wealth; and, though long familiarity with Turkish animosity has taught them the folly of ostentation, they house and clothe themselves in comfort and present an appearance of stable and admirable citizenship.

Being, as they undoubtedly are, the absolute sinew of the state, it is a natural question: Why is this thing being done to them? Nobody knows.

Ninety percent of all the business in the big towns on the Black Sea, and, indeed, all through Asia Minor, has been in the hands of Armenians, and their banishment has paralyzed the industrial life of the country. Removals may be made swiftly enough, but orderly confiscation of property and reorganization are slower processes. And those who know say the Turk is absolutely incapable of taking the place in the business life of the country the Armenian has so long occupied, to the country's very marked advantage. The colossal stupidity of it is its most inexplicable feature.

The proclamation speaks of "places which have been prepared in the interior vilayets." No preparation of any kind was ever made, so far as I could learn. The points to which the exiles are sent are to the southward, in the Arabian Desert, along the middle reaches of the Euphrates and in Mesopotamia.

One terrible account came through about eight hundred women and children who were separated from their husbands and fathers, and, with only a few old men among them, were started on a forty-five days' march from their home town to Aleppo, one of the big concentration centers. There were women of culture and refinement among them, who were forced, as the hardier peasants were, to carry on their backs all the necessaries to sustain life on the journey. They were in charge of Turkish gendarmes, whose instructions with regard to them seemed to include nothing about protection. Children were born on the way and the sick women were forced immediately to march on. One woman fell by the road side in the throes of labor, only to be prodded by the bayonet of a gendarme, who said there was "no time for anything like that." This was reported by an eyewitness. She died and her body was abandoned.

One man wrote in August: "The roads to the south are strewn and stenched with rotting bodies, and the streams are clogged with them. Despairing mothers—insane, of course— throw their infants into the rivers or leave them in the camps to die. Women give up everything they possess—-jewels, money, their very clothes and coverings—to buy immunity."

The women who are separated from their men and sent alone to the place of exile are promised that their men will rejoin them, will be marched on more rapidly to prepare places for them; but it seldom happens so. The men, by thousands, have been raided and massacred—"lost" by the way. One Armenian writes: "The purpose is our utter destruction. The Turks say so themselves. Destruction concealed from the world, cold-blooded, calculating! And methods are cunningly contrived to get from us at once all the money we have. We may buy our lives for the time being, but when our means are exhausted we die."

The Concentration Camps

At Ada Bazar there has long been established a concentration camp for about forty thousand people. Each family is given a small space, about eight by eight feet; and in this space every act of life must be performed. The camp is heavily guarded and no Armenian, unarmed and helpless though he be, is allowed outside its boundaries. This is not written about something that happened once on a time, but about something that is happening now. As you read these lines that camp exists. Your mind may dwell on it as one of the countless horrors the bitter winter wind is playing upon to-day in a heretofore comparatively happy world.

But how do these people live? Food and water venders demand exorbitant prices. For the rest one's imagination may give itself free rein. Exaggeration of miserable details is hardly possible. They are concentrated at Ada Bazar for deportation to remote points as rapidly as the authorities can handle them. They are transported in box cars on the Baghdad Railroad and the railroad running east from Smyrna as far as is possible; then come the weary marches. There is an added touch of irony, too, in the fact that everybody is made to pay railroad fare.

There were a number of women teachers and students from one of the American mission schools who were gathered up and sent to a point far down on the Baghdad Railroad from which they expected to be marched south into Mesopotamia. The American ambassador, whose unceasing efforts in behalf of the Armenians would move heaven and earth if heaven and earth could be moved, entered a warm protest against this, and followed it up with sufficient pressure to induce Talat Bey to promise that they should be sent back to their school. Under orders joyfully obeyed they got on a train and returned to Ada Bazar, only to find when they got there that there had been a change of the official mind. They were immediately ordered back to where they came from, and were made to pay for the journey the third time.

The great dispersal began out on the eastern border and in the Black Sea cities, but it moved very rapidly in the direction of Constantinople, until it embraced the whole of Asia Minor. American consuls and businessmen everywhere have seconded the splendid efforts of the Ambassador to mitigate the sufferings of the people in some degree, but their action has been met with threats of violence against themselves.

One young North Carolinian, representative of a large American concern with ramifications throughout the world, was arrested, treated with an entire lack of consideration and sent to Constantinople. The authorities assured him they would confiscate the valuable stores in his large warehouses, but his characteristic American answer was: "All right; there they are." When I saw him last, nothing had happened. He had committed no offense, he was merely in the way of contemplated large operations which they did not want him to see; so he was deported to Constantinople.

Talat Bey promised that Constantinople should not be touched. He even gave an intelligent reason, based on expediency, why it should not be touched. Tranquility in the capital and an orderly continuance of the city's business routine were too important to the situation to be disturbed for the time being; but something happened to change the Ministerial mind.

They began by gathering up the Armenians in Constantinople at the rate of about fifty a day, and among the first to go were many of the teachers and servants from the American schools. Nearly everybody one knew had lost or was in danger of losing some friend or valued retainer. The gatekeepers and watchmen at the Embassies and other foreign establishments were gathered up and sent into the interior regardless of the fact that they were men who could not be replaced.

1 went with a party of friends a few days before I left to explore in a thorough manner the seventh-century Walls of Heraclius, from the Golden Horn up round the site of the ancient Palace of Blachemae and on to Adrianople Gate. With us was a British clergyman who has been in Constantinople for a great many years, and who has a detailed and accurate knowledge of the city's history, which he is able and willing to impart in a manner to make such an expedition in his company a rare privilege. We were having a memorably pleasant afternoon.

We had followed a winding course for an hour or more through towers and underground passages, over crumbling ruins and past long, perfectly preserved stretches of the glorious old battlemented structure, when we came to a little wooden gate through which the reverend doctor said we must pass to get into the Tower of Anemas.

Mary Anderson Bereft

"And now," said the doctor, "we are going to see Mary Anderson. Mary is so ugly that the name was suggested to me by acute contrast; but she has a rare smile, Mary has, and I always like to see her, because she cheers me up."

He pulled a cord, which rang a little tinkling bell off somewhere behind the low house beyond the gateway, and pretty soon Mary came and admitted us.

She was trying hard to smile, but the tears were coursing down her poor old wrinkled face and she was sobbing under the most pitiful efforts at self-control ever witnessed.

"In goodness' name, what's the matter, Mary?" exclaimed the doctor.

Then she gave up and frankly wept, wept bitterly.

"They have just taken my son," she said; "he left not twenty minutes ago. If you had only been here! Maybe they would have let him stay for you. They took his father only last week, and I don't know where either of them has gone."

She spoke Turkish, which the doctor translated for us as she talked. She was left entirely alone, with no means of support, and she had no idea what was to become of her. She only knew that in all probability she had seen the last of both her husband and son, and she plaintively emphasized the fact that she was not given the comfort of having them taken at the same time, so that she might know they were together.

The worst of it is that such poor Armenians are not able to pay their way and in consequence their sufferings are increased a thousandfold. They are given neither food nor clothing, except by their fellow exiles, and they are not permitted to do anything to earn a living until they reach their destination. Does not the proclamation say "If they are sheltered or given food and assistance the persons who thus shelter or aid them shall be sent before the Court-Martial for execution"? This is meant to apply only to those who "refrain from leaving or seek to hide themselves"; but fear makes it applicable to all. Everywhere they are shunned as death's-heads.

*****

After the French Revolution happened in 1789, England was terrified of popular revolts coming to her own shores. As a result, efforts were made to obviate this threat by giving the people more political power.

In 1861, John Stuart Mill wrote "Considerations on Representative Government," wherein he compares society to a pyramid. He wrote that a just society that saw to the needs of its people was akin to a pyramid on a broad base. By contrast, an oligarchy, which only served the The Few, was like an inverted pyramid balancing precariously on its tip. As a result, it was unstable and given to collapse.

Mill therefore believed that, in response to the French Revolution, England had acted correctly in expanding the vote to men from the poor and middle classes. But, as a progressive, he believed that the reforms didn't go far enough. He wrote, "In the preceding argument for universal but graduated suffrage, I have taken no account of difference of sex. I consider it to be as entirely irrelevant to political rights as difference in height or in the color of the hair. All human beings have the same interest in good government; the welfare of all is alike affected by it, and they have equal need of a voice in it to secure their share of its benefits."

Though he was making these statements in the mid-nineteenth century, it was not until after World War One that women were finally granted the vote—but initially only on a partial basis. It came through the "Representation of the People Act of 1918," which only allowed women aged thirty and above to vote. (The voting age wouldn't be lowered for women until 1928, when females twenty-one and above could finally vote.)

The United States would extend the vote to women in 1920. In Germany, it was 1918; in Russia, it was 1917. Neutral Switzerland didn't grant women the right to vote until 1971 (with some cantons not extending them the right until 1990), demonstrating that war indeed accelerates social change. Those countries that abstained from war (like Switzerland) maintained their older culture and traditions for a much longer period of time.

As a result of these sociological variables, tensions arose between the suffragettes themselves. Some were vehemently pro-war, while others had grown war-weary as years of attrition had made them question the wisdom of the current system.

Clare Stobart wrote, "The more 'natural' it seems for man

to fight his fellow-man, in order to acquire supremacy, the more urgent it is for society to intervene. . . . Society has failed in its primary function of preserving life. But society has hitherto been controlled by men only. . . . Nature, in her beneficence, generally arranges that side by side with the poisonous plant, the antidote shall grow, and thus, side by side with the growth of militarism, has also grown the women's movement."

Not all feminists were pacifists, however. Emmeline Pankhurst demanded "women's right to serve," and said that females had a greater role to play than just knitting socks and buying war bonds. She and her daughter, Christabel, had started the Women's Social and Political Union in 1903. At the outbreak of war in 1914, the government made a bargain with them. They would release all suffragettes from prison (due to publicity stunts they had previously engaged in such as blocking traffic and breaking windows) and pay them £2,000 if they supported the war effort and encouraged men to enlist.

One of the programs that they aided the British Ministry of Propaganda with was a strategy to encourage men to enlist in the armed forces by shaming civilian males by handing them a white feather. (These were usually chicken feathers, with women running up to a man, handing him a feather and taunting, "What a chicken you are!") This practice, commonly known as the White Feather Campaign, became a powerful, unofficial extension of the British propaganda machine, exploiting social norms around masculinity, duty, and shame.

Along with Emmeline Pankhurst, another "Emmeline" participated in this campaign: Emmeline Pethick-Lawrence, of the United Suffragists.

Other feminists were mortified at the idea of their movement being subverted into being an instrument of State power, and instead promoted pacifism.

In April, 1915, for instance, a summit took place in the Hague, where 1,000 women converged to attend the first International Congress of Women. Among the activists calling for an end to war were American peace activist Jane Addams, Dutch physician Aletta Jacobs, German trade union activist Lisa Gustava Heymann, and Hungarian journalist Rosika Schwimmer. The two main goals of the conference were to make governments aware of the harm done to women and children by war, and the assertion that women's suffrage should be adopted.

Mary Chamberlain (1888 – 1938), writing for *The Survey* in their June 5, 1915 edition, submitted the following article on the conference:

The four of us sat over coffee in the cafe of the Hotel Central in The Hague.

Soldiers in peaked caps, loitering with their sweethearts, passed the window; bicyclists zigzagged dangerously through the crowd: and once in a while, the last bit of Dutch picturesqueness—the wooden shoes, flaring white head-dress and gold hair-pins of a peasant woman, kept us aware that this black-coated orthodox stream of passers-by was not the ebb and flow of Broadway. Inside, the vermilion trimmings and gold braid of smart uniforms gave color to the stodgy gathering of Dutch folk, and a jolly American ragtime, though bereft of the American cafe dance-floor, lightened the heavy menu of fish and meats and compotes.

The International Congress of Women was over. The four of us were journalists—tired with taking notes, seeking interviews, hurrying to meetings, straining our ears to foreign languages. We were in danger of losing sight of the spirit of the congress in our zeal to "get a story" from some delegate, in our efforts to straighten out names and numbers and speeches. Now for the first time we were trying to touch this spirit and to clear our vision by an exchange of impressions.

"It was bourgeois," said the Socialist, "a gathering of senti-mentalists. The real people who want the war stopped are the working people and they would have nothing to do with this congress. To me it seemed barren and cold. Why. I've heard a little East Side striker rouse a meeting to a pitch of enthusiasm that was never touched by those clubwomen and suffrage leaders."

"Self-control, you mean, not lack of feeling," objected the short story writer. "I felt a great swell of emotion under the reserve of those women from warring nations. Constraint was necessary or it would have burst on the meeting like a shower of shrapnel."

"And as for the delegates from neutral countries," added the newspaper woman, "I'm sure the minds of many of those women were poisoned for the first time with the fear of war. For the first time I believe that hundreds of Dutch women in that audience realized that war would mean the flowers of Holland soaked with the blood of the recruits drilling there in front of the Dierentium where the congress met."

From the press-table of the congress back to America, to England, to Germany, to Scandinavia. I knew criticisms had gone as diverse as these. With them had gone others less honest, less intelligent, more partisan. The newspapers of the countries from which the delegates came denounced the congress as "pro-German," as traitorous, as hysterical, as base and silly. Some people claimed an influence for the congress far wider than it can attain for years, others decried it as futile.

Bewildered by this wrangle and confusion. I left my friends in the cafe and went to Jane Addams to ask her opinion of the congress. For three days Miss Addams had, as president, steered the business of the congress through a sea of resolutions, amendments and suggestions given her in French, German, English and Dutch. She was thoroughly acquainted with the hitches and obstacles that clog every international conference and had been most closely in touch with the members of the congress.

"The great achievement of this congress," said Miss Addams thoughtfully, "is to my mind the getting together of these women from all parts of Europe, when their men-folks are shooting each other from opposite trenches. When in every warring country there is such a wonderful awakening of national consciousness flowing from heart to heart, it is a supreme effort of heroism to rise to the feeling of internationalism, without losing patriotism."

With a rush of tenderness and sympathy I remembered some of the women who sat beside Miss Addams on the platform at the congress—frail little Miss Courtney and Chrystal Macmillan. British to the fiber yet offering a hearty second to many resolutions proposed by German delegates; Lida Gustava Heymann, whose honest straightforward ways made one smile at the insinuation of a congress packed with German spies; valiant Eugenie Hamer, who pushed through from Belgium with five companions; warm-hearted Rosika Schwimmer from Hungary; and Frau Leopoldine Kulka of Austria, with her quiet blue eyes and patient face.

Nearly everyone of those women who sat there side by side so dignified and courteous, had brothers, husbands or friends facing each other in maddened fury or even now mown down by each other's bullets. It was a great test of courage for these women to risk the bitterness of their families, the ridicule of their friends and the censure of their governments to come to this international woman's congress. In the midst of the war tumult which is making all Europe shake, it meant a far sweep of imagination to realize that the feelings of mothers, sisters and wives are the same in all countries and it took the finest generosity for these women to associate themselves in a discussion of means to restore international good will.

The congress that bore this fruit was planned with doubt and misgivings. When the International Alliance for Women Suffrage held its last congress at Budapest in June, 1913, it was decided to hold the next convention at Berlin in June, 1915. Meanwhile the war broke out, kindling its hatred between nations and burning away all thought of an international suffrage gathering. However, a few broadminded women still held fast to their ideals in the midst of these rough realities. Among them, the Dutch National Committee for International Interests, a sub-division of the Alliance for Women Suffrage, ventured to lift up its voice. It proposed that the congress which it was impossible to hold at Berlin should be convoked instead in the Netherlands.

The twenty-six separate countries affiliated with the international alliance were approached, but the answers received were on the whole discouraging. The idea itself met with general favor but it was considered advisable to refrain from holding official assemblies. Therefore, the only chance of success lay in separately consulting the prominent women of the different countries, both belligerent and neutral.

This consultation took place with the result that a meeting was held on February 12-13 in Amsterdam, attended by a number of British, German, Dutch and Belgian women. Here the plans for the International Congress of Women were laid, the preliminary program was drawn, invitations were sent out, committees appointed and the emphasis of the congress turned from political equality to peace.

The next difficulty in the path of the congress confronted, not the central committee at The Hague but those who desired to take part in the conference. It was one thing for these women to accept the invitation to the congress; it was another for them to reach Holland. Of 180 British women accepting the invitation to the congress, two only arrived—Kathleen Courtney and Chrystal Macmillan, English suffragists and members of the International Committee on Resolutions, who reached The Hague a week before the congress opened. The other 178 were first pared down to 24 by the secretary for Foreign Affairs, who advised the Home Office to limit the issuance of passports. Reginald McKenna, British secretary of state for Home Affairs, has explained this action by stating that his colleague in the Department for Foreign Affairs believed that so large a number of English women in a city near to the scene of war and infested with the enemy's spies would constitute a danger for the country. Therefore 24 delegates were sorted out, representing the most important organizations and seeming most prudent in giving out information. In doing this, Mr. McKenna was careful to make it understood that these delegates had received no official character.

The reason for the non-appearance of these twenty-four picked delegates is not quite so clear and must be explained as the "fortunes of war." When a member of parliament who objected to the participation of English women in the congress, asked Mr. McKenna if any of the twenty-four had actually reached The Hague, the secretary replied: "No, indeed. You know that all communication between England and Holland was interrupted after the delegates received their passports."

But while these twenty-four women were waiting at Folkstone for any sort of boat to convey them to Holland, Miss Courtney and Miss Macmillan were making up in quality of membership what England lacked in quantity. It was the hard work and perseverance of these two women that made one almost forget the small proportion of delegates from this allied nation in the membership of the congress. One Canadian delegate, Laura Hughes of Toronto, crossed the Atlantic to represent the colonies.

The action of the British government in suspending traffic between England and Holland was also responsible for nearly cutting off the American contingent from the congress. For four days the steamship Noordam, loaded with ammunition for the Dutch government in the hold, and with forty-two peace delegates to the Dutch capital in the first cabin, lay at anchor off Diel. The delegates sent telegrams to the American ambassador at London and the American consul at Dover; they held meetings to devise ways and means to investigate the halt; finally, they settled down to face the fact that they were as nothing compared to the transference of troops to France or the movements of the British fleet. Then just as mysteriously as she had been delayed, the Noordam was ordered to proceed, and we reached Rotterdam without meeting mines or further mishaps, the very day the congress opened.

Much has been said by the press and critics of the congress of the "Germanizing" of this peace meeting. The thirty German delegates and the fifteen Austrians and Hungarians present have been called the "Kaiser's cat's-paws," German spies and many other names. It has been suggested that the German and Austro-Hungarian governments were only too glad to be represented at a peace meeting; it has even been hinted that the expenses of the congress were met by German government funds. Strangely enough, the newspapers of a country from which a large number of delegates were excluded by government orders—Great Britain,—were loudest in proclaiming that the congress was steamrollered by the Germans!

As a matter of fact, the way of the German, Austrian and Hungarian delegates was not altogether paved with ease and cordiality. Although they finally received their passports without trouble, they were at first suspected by their governments and at all times they have been the butt of ridicule and calumny of the press and the general public. The union of German women, for example, has almost unanimously denounced the participation of German women in the congress.

All the delegates openly declared that they did not represent the sentiment of the majority of women in their fatherlands, but only small, radical groups. Among them are women whose names are well known to the international Suffrage Alliance and in social work. Anita Augspurg and Lida G. Heymann of Munich, are founders of the suffrage movement in Germany; Helene Stocker and Fraulein Rotten of Berlin are, respectively, president of the League for the Protection of Mothers, and an officer of the League for the Care of Prisoners; Rosika Schwimmer of Hungary, represented the Association of Agricultural Woman Laborers, a suffrage organization of peasant women; Vilma G. Giicklich and Paula Pogany, are the president and secretary of the Hungarian Feminist Alliance; Anna Zipemowsky is a member of the Hungarian Peace Association; Leopoldine Kulka and Olga Misar came as delegates of the Austrian Women's Union (suffrage); Bertha Frölich, as delegate of the Society of Temperance women; and Darynska Golinska came from Austrian Poland with a memorial from the suffering Polish women demanding the rebuilding of an independent Poland as an "indispensable reservation" in a lasting peace.

Likewise Rosa Genoni of Milan, lecturer, writer, and the sole delegate from Italy, did not claim to represent the widespread feeling of her country-women. "The other women in Italy," said Madame Genoni, "were frightened to cross Germany to Holland, for they fear in Italy that war may break out any minute. Alas! in Italy they do not think only of peace. Everybody desires it perhaps, but first of all they think of national interest. Even the peace associations in Italy are drawn into the mesh of war."

From the Scandinavian countries came large delegations to the congress, representing in most instances the committees formed in these northern nations for the international congress. Among them stood out such names as Anna Lindhagen of Sweden, inspector of children's institutions and one of the seven women members of the town council of Stockholm; and Thora Daugaard of Denmark, representing 15,000 suffragists.

No Russian or French woman attended the congress. Whereas the European press overlooked much that was of real and lasting importance in the Congress, few papers failed to publish in full the manifesto of the *Conseil National des Femmes Francises* and *L'Union pour le Suffrage des Femmes*, organizations representing more than 150,000 French women. The manifesto is addressed "to the women of neutral and allied countries." It is a touching document courteously declining for French women a share in the congress and proudly declaring that "in order that future generations may reap the fruit of this magnificent display of self-sacrifice and death, French women will bear the conflict as long as it will be necessary. At this time united with those who battle and die, they do not know how to talk of peace."

The manifesto further proposes that French women can talk of peace only when justice has been triumphantly vindicated by the heroic defenders of the French nation.

In spite of this manifesto many letters were received from individual French women telling their desire to reach the congress and of the impossibility of traveling so far. Among them was a telegram of sympathy from Jules Siegfried, president of the *Conseil National des Femmes Franchises*, and a letter signed by Mme. Duchene, Chairman of the *Section du Travail du Conseil National* and by some fifteen working women, which offered to "the women of other nations good wishes and assurance that we are ready to work with them more ardently than ever to prepare the 'peace of tomorrow.'"

Russian women sent a letter expressing much the same sentiment as did the French manifesto, but the very feeling which kept these French and Russian women from the congress drove five valiant little Belgian women across the border into Holland from devastated Belgium. Eugene Hamer and Mlle. Sarton, vice-president and treasurer of *L'Alliance Belge des Femmes pour la Paix par l'Education*, decided that no peace congress attended by German and Austrian delegates should pass resolutions without a hearing before Belgian women. They determined not to vote but to protest against any measure, such as the calling of an armistice, which they deemed unjust to their country.

With three companions they obtained permission from the German authorities to go. They went by automobile to Esschen, where they were searched to the skin; thence they walked for two hours to Rosendahl across the Dutch border, and from there they traveled to The Hague by train. Then, when Mlle. Hamer and her friends at last reached the congress, it was Dr. Augspurg of Munich who welcomed them to a seat on the platform.

So, over seas and mountains, pushing aside dangers and obstacles, more than three hundred women "got together" with the Dutch delegates and visitors who crowded the meetings night after night. However any might criticize the proceedings of the congress, none could fail to admire the magnificent spirit of these women who dared clasp hands with women from an enemy country. Even if this international Congress wields little influence, it was, as Miss Addams said, a lasting achievement in thus uniting from every corner of Europe different sympathies and beliefs in one great yearning for peace.

But as I talked with Miss Addams, another thought came into my mind. Was it not, I asked her, a higher test of courage than "getting together" when the trenches were bleeding with wounded comrades, to "stick together" until out of their common suffering these women evolved a charter of common aspiration? Someone in the cafe had spoken of a mutual distrust that seemed to constrain the delegates. Now, talking with Miss Addams, I realized how this mistrust had gradually melted. Like my Socialist friend, I missed the flare of passion which kindles a meeting held to score a specific wrong; I revolted sometimes at dodging realities and floating in a cloud of theories: I, too, missed the vigorous robust solidarity of a congress bound together by the sense of the inter-dependence of labor. But more and more I was feeling that strong, sober solidarity based on universal mourning.

"Everybody talks about victory," said Rosika Schwimmer in one of her stirring speeches, "but we women know; that every victory means the death of thousands of sons of other mothers."

It was grief and sympathy that welded us together.

At the first session of the congress, without a dissenting voice a motion was carried making the basis of membership in the congress the acceptance of two resolutions—that women shall be granted equal political rights with men and that future international disputes shall be subject to conciliation and arbitration.

With the meeting-ground of the congress thus defined, the way was left open for debate and discussion on any other resolution to be considered. But so great was the unity of feeling that day after day of conferences slid by with no or little friction. Indeed, the monotony of perfect accord caused us at the press table to snatch and overemphasize the faintest spark of sensationalism—the harangue, for instance, of the militant suffragette who vowed that for every woman in England wishing to attend the peace congress 1,000 wished to fight: or the excitement of a Belgian lady who thought that the phrase "backward nations" referred to Belgium. Many resolutions were passed unanimously such as those protesting against women's sufferings in war. Demanding democratic control of foreign policy, urging that the education of children be directed toward peace and that women be represented in the conference of powers after the war. Even the radical resolutions introduced by the American contingent went through without protest. Among these were resolutions calling for open seas and free trade routes, for the acceptance of the principle that investments in a foreign country be made at the risk of the investor, for mediation without armistice and for the establishment of a permanent international conference which shall deal with practical proposals for future international co-operation and shall appoint a permanent council of conciliation for the settlement of differences arising from social and economic causes.

From the German delegates came a resolution of even greater import which repudiates the right of conquest. This resolution affirms that there shall be no transference of territory without the consent of the residents and urges that autonomy and a democratic parliament shall not be refused to any people.

When the resolution came up for vote advocating universal disarmament and urging all countries to take over the manufacture of arms and munitions of war and to control international traffic in the same, a stir was created by a delegate from the United States who moved an amendment that "traffic in arms from neutral countries be prohibited."

Miss Addams ruled the amendment out of order as bearing upon present conditions, but added that she herself as an American citizen favored it.

Aside from the delay and slight confusion caused by tedious translation, there was but one hitch in the proceedings of the congress. It came after Madame Schwimmer's appeal for women to "call a thunderous halt *tomorrow* that shall overthrow the thunder of the trenches." By a rising vote the congress had voted to accept without debate this resolution urging the governments of the world to put an end to bloodshed and to begin peace negotiations. Then Mlle. Hamer, burning with the spirit of the French manifesto, pleaded for a peace based on justice "which would return to Belgium her liberty, independence, richness and prosperity." Unanimously the congress voted to insert in this most important of resolutions:

"The congress demands that the peace which follows shall be permanent and therefore based on principles of justice."

Thus "arbitration" bridged the one division of feeling in the congress which threatened a serious split.

What will come of it all?

That is what the world of practical people, who demand immediate results, is asking. When I questioned my Socialist friend, she scoffed a little bitterly, "A lot of talk that will blow away with the delegates." But the newspaper woman reflected that it would leave its stamp on the woman movement in every country, and the magazine writer declared that its end was already attained in dispelling the idea of implacable hatred between women of warring countries.

The one immediate step of the congress was to delegate envoys, women from both neutral and belligerent nations, to carry the message expressed in the congress resolutions to combatants and non-combatant countries. Already Jane Addams, Aletta H. Jacobs, chairman of the executive committee of the congress, and Rosa Genoni of Italy, have been received by the court of Holland, have presented the resolutions to the prime minister of England and have come back to the continent in a tour which includes the capitals of Germany, Belgium, France and Austria. They will later be joined by Kathleen Courtney of England and Anita Augspurg of Germany, and will visit the neutral countries of Switzerland, Spain and United States. The entrance of Italy into the war will prevent these delegates visiting Rome as planned.

Meanwhile another group has been appointed to go to Denmark, Sweden, Norway, and Russia.

To students of diplomacy and to the "practical" people of the world the expeditions will seem, like the congress itself, the action of visionaries. They will laugh at a "parcel of women" bearing resolutions to prime ministers who are vexed with the burdens of war. They will sneer at its futility and assail its temerity. But to others, and especially to us who attended the congress, the mission of these women will mean that the spirit of the congress will not be girded by the canals of Holland but will reach across trenches smoking with war.

*****

Mary Roberts Rinehart (1876 – 1958) is often referred to as the "American Agatha Christie," though her literary career predated Christie's by over a decade. She was one of the most successful and influential writers in the early 20th century, primarily recognized for her contributions to the mystery genre. (She coined the term "The butler did it!")

Magazine editors naturally clamored for her to work for them in the capacity of a war correspondent. (They knew readers were bored by the dry, statistics-based writing of most male war correspondents, which largely restricted itself to military strategy and munitions numbers, and wanted the more humanizing character-sketching that female war correspondents were known for.)

When the *Saturday Evening Post* got her to write for them, it was considered a coup. Here is her report from May 8, 1915:

Until now our excursions to the trenches, aside from the discomfort of the weather and the mud, had been fairly safe, although there was always the chance of a shell. To that now was to be added a fresh hazard—the sniping that goes on all night long.

Our car moved quietly for a mile, paralleling the trenches. Then it stopped. The rest of the journey was to be on foot.

All traces of the storm had passed, except for the pools of mud which, gleaming like small lakes, filled shell holes in the road. An ammunition lorry had drawn up in the shadow of a hedge and was cautiously unloading. Evidently the night's movement of troops was over, for the roads were empty.

A few feet beyond the lorry we came up to the trenches. We were behind them, only head and shoulders above. There was no sign of life or movement, except for the silent *fusées* that burst occasionally a little to our right. Walking was bad. The Belgian blocks of the road were coated with slippery mud, and from long use and erosion the stones themselves were rounded, so that our feet slipped over them. At the right was a shallow ditch three or four feet wide. Beyond that the railway embankment where, as Captain Fastrez had explained, the Belgian Army had taken up its position after being driven back across the Yser.

The embankment loomed shoulder high, and between it and the ditch were the trenches. There was no sound from them, but sentries halted us frequently. On such occasions the party stopped abruptly—for here sentries are apt to fire first and investigate afterward—and one officer advanced with the password. There is always something grim and menacing about the attitude of the sentry as he waits on such occasions. His carbine is not over his shoulder, but in his hands, ready for use. The bayonet gleams. His eyes are fixed watchfully on the advance. A false move, and his overstrained nerves may send the carbine to his shoulder.

The House Barrier

We walked just behind the trenches in the moonlight for a mile. No one said anything. The wind was icy. Across the railroad embankment it chopped the inundation into small crested waves. Only by putting one's head down was it possible to battle ahead. From Dixmude came the intermittent red flashes of guns. But the trenches beside us were entirely silent.

At the end of a mile we stopped. The road turned abruptly to the right and crossed the railroad embankment, and at this crossing was the ruin of what had been the House of the Barrier, where in peaceful times the crossing tender lived.

It had been almost destroyed. The side towards the German lines was indeed a ruin, but one room was fairly whole. However, the door had been shot away. To enter, it was necessary to lift away an extemporized one of planks roughly nailed together, which leaned against the aperture.

The moving of the door showed more firelight, and a very small, shaded and smoky lamp on a stand. There were officers here again. The little house is slightly in advance of the trenches, and once inside it was possible to realize its exposed position. Standing as it does on the elevation of the railroad, it is constantly under fire. It is surrounded by barbed wire and flanked by trenches in which are mitrailleuses.

The walls were full of shell holes, stuffed with sacks of straw or boarded over. What had been windows were now jagged openings, similarly closed. The wind came through steadily, smoking the chimney of the lamp and making the flame flicker.

There was one chair.

I wish I could go farther. I wish I could say that shells were bursting overhead, and that I sat calmly in the one chair and made notes. I sat, true enough, but I sat because I was tired and my feet were wet. And instead of making notes I examined my new six-guinea silk rubber rain cape for barbed wire tears. Not a shell came near. The German battery across had ceased firing at dusk that evening, and was playing pinochle four hundred yards away across the inundation. The snipers were writing letters home.

It is true that at any time an artillery man might lose a game and go out and fire a gun to vent his spleen or to keep his hand in. And the snipers might begin to notice that the rain was over, and that there was suspicious activity at the House of the Barrier. And, to take away the impression of perfect peace, big guns were busy just north and south of us. Also, just where we were the Germans had made a terrific charge three nights before to capture an outpost. But the fact remains that I brought away not even a bullet hole through the crown of my soft felt hat.

When I had been thawed out they took me into the trenches. Because of the inundation directly in front, they are rather shallow, and at this point were built against the railroad embankment with earth, boards, and here and there a steel rail from the track. Some of them were covered, too, but not with bomb proof material. The tops were merely shelters from the rain and biting wind. The men lay or sat in them—it was impossible to stand. Some of them were like tiny houses into which the men crawled from the rear, and by placing a board, which served as a door, managed to keep out at least a part of the bitter wind.

Evening in the Trench

In the first trench I was presented to a bearded major. He was lying flat and apologized for not being able to rise. There was a machine gun beside him. He told me with some pride that it was an American gun, and that it never jammed. When a machine gun jams the man in charge of it dies and his comrades die, and things happen with great rapidity. On the other side of him was a cat, curled up and sound asleep. There was a telephone instrument there. It was necessary to step over the wire that was strung upon the ground.

All night long he lies there with his gun, watching for the first movement in the trenches across. For here, near the House of the Barrier, has taken place some of the most furious fighting of this part of the line.

In the next division of the trench were three men. They were cleaning and oiling their rifles round a candle. The surprise of all of these men at seeing a woman was almost absurd. Word went down the trenches that a woman was visiting. Heads popped out and cautious comments were made. It was concluded that I was visiting royalty, but the excitement died when it was discovered that I was not the Queen. Now and then, when a trench looked clean and dry, I was invited in. It was necessary to get down and crawl in on hands and knees.

Here was a man warming his hands over a tiny fire kindled in a tin pail. He had bored holes in the bottom of the pail for air, and was shielding the glow carefully with his overcoat.

Many people have written about the trenches—the mud, the odors, the inhumanity of compelling men to live under such foul conditions. Nothing that they have said can be too strong. Under the best conditions the life is ghastly, horrible, impossible.

That night, when from a semishielded position I could look across to the German line, the contrast between the condition of the men in the trenches and the beauty of the scenery was appalling. In each direction, as far as one could see, lay a gleaming lagoon of water. The moon made a silver path across it, and here and there on its borders were broken and twisted winter trees.

"It is beautiful," said Captain Fastrez beside me, in a low voice.

"But it is full of the dead. They are taken out whenever it is possible, but it is not often possible."

"And when there is an attack the attacking side must go through the water?"

"Not always, but in many places."

"What will happen if it freezes over?"

He explained that it was salt water, and would not freeze easily. And the cold of that part of the country is not the cold of America in the same latitude. It is not a cold of low temperature; it is a damp, penetrating cold that goes through garments of every weight and seems to chill the very blood in a man's body.

"How deep is the water?" I asked.

"It varies—from two to eight feet. Here it is shallow."

"I should think they would come over."

"The water is full of barbed wire," he said grimly. "And some, a great many, have tried—and failed."

As of the trenches, many have written of the stenches of this war. But the odor of that beautiful lagoon was horrible. I do not care to emphasize it. It is one of the things best forgotten. But any lingering belief I may have had in the grandeur and glory of war died that night beside that silver lake—died of an odor, and will never live again.

And now came a discussion.

The road crossing the railroad embankment turned sharply

to the left and proceeded in front of the trenches. There was no shelter on that side of the embankment. The inundation bordered the road, and just beyond the inundation were the German trenches.

There were no trees, no shrubbery, no houses; just a flat road, paved with Belgian blocks, that gleamed in the moonlight.

At last the decision was made. We would go along the road, provided I realized from the first that it was dangerous. One or two could walk there with a good chance for safety, but not more. The little group had been augmented. It must break up; two might walk together, and then two a safe distance behind. Four would certainly be fired on.

I wanted to go. It was not a matter of courage. I had simply, parrot-fashion, mimicked the attitude of mind of the officers. One after another I had seen men go into danger with a shrug of the shoulders.

"If it comes it comes!" they said, and went on. So I, too, had become a fatalist. If I was to be shot it would happen, if I had to buy a rifle and try to clean it myself to fulfill my destiny.

The Sentry Agreement

So they let me go. I went farther than they expected, as it turned out. There was a great deal of indignation and relief when it was over. But that is later on.

A very tall Belgian officer took me in charge. It was necessary to work through a barbed-wire barricade, twisting and turning through its mazes. The moonlight helped. It was at once a comfort and an anxiety, for it seemed to me that my khaki-colored suit gleamed in it. The Belgian officers in their dark blue were less conspicuous. I thought they had an unfair advantage of me, and that it was idiotic of the British to wear and advocate anything so absurd as khaki. My cape ballooned like a sail in the wind. I felt at least double my ordinary size, and that even a sniper with a squint could hardly miss me. And, by way of comfort, I had one last instruction before I started:

"If *a fusée* goes up, stand perfectly still. If you move they will fire."

The entire safety of the excursion depended on a sort of tacit agreement that, in part at least, obtains as to sentries.

This is a new warfare, one of artillery, supported by infantry in trenches. And it has been necessary to make new laws for it. The winter deadlock has given rise to one of the most curious. It is a sort of *modus vivendi* by which each side protects its own sentries by leaving the enemy's sentries unmolested so long as there is no active fighting. They are always in plain view before the trenches. In case of a charge they are the first to be shot, of course. But long winter nights and days have gone by along certain parts of the front where the hostile trenches are close together, and the sentries, keeping their monotonous lookout, have been undisturbed.

No doubt by the time this article is published the situation will have changed to a certain extent; there will be more active fighting, larger bodies of men will be involved. The spring floods south of the inundation will have dried up. No Man's Land will have ceased to be a swamp and the deadlock will be broken.

But on that February night I put my faith in this agreement and it held.

The tall Belgian officer asked me if I was frightened. I said I was not. This was not the truth; but it was no time for the truth.

"They are not shooting," I said. "It looks perfectly safe."

He shrugged his shoulders and glanced toward the German trenches. "They have been sleeping during the rain," he said briefly. "But when one of them wakes up, look out!"

After that there was little conversation, and what there was was in whispers.

As we proceeded the stench from the beautiful moonlit water grew overpowering. The officer told me the reason.

A little farther along a path of fascines had been built out over the inundation to an outpost halfway to the German trenches. The building of this narrow roadway had cost many lives.

Half a mile along the road we were sharply challenged by a sentry. When he had received the password he stood back and let us pass. Alone, in that bleak and exposed position, always in full view as he paced back and forward, carbine on shoulder, with not even a tree trunk or a hedge for shelter, the first to go at the whim of some German sniper or at any indication of an attack, he was a pathetic, almost a tragic, figure. He looked very young too. I stopped and asked him in a whisper how old he was.

He said he was nineteen!

He may have been. I know something about boys, and I think he was seventeen at the most. There are plenty of boys of that age doing just what that lad was doing.

Afterward I learned that it was no part of the original plan to take a woman over the fascine path to the outpost; that Captain Fastrez ground his teeth in impotent rage when he saw where I was being taken. But it was not possible to call or even to come up to us. So, blithely and unconsciously the tall Belgian officer and I turned to the right, and I was innocently on my way to the German trenches.

After a little I realized that this was rather more war than I had expected. The fascines were slippery; the path only four or five feet wide. On each side was the water, hideous with many secrets.

I stopped, a third of the way out, and looked back. It looked about as dangerous in one direction as another. So we went on. Once I slipped and fell. And now, looming out of the moonlight, I could see the outpost which was the object of our visit.

I have always been grateful to that Belgian lieutenant for his mistake. Just how grateful I might have been had anything untoward happened, I cannot say. But the excursion was worth all the risk, and more.

The Soldier Monk in His Tower

On a bit of high ground stands what was once the tiny hamlet of Oudstuyvenskerke—the ruins of two small white houses and the tower of the destroyed church—hardly a tower anymore, for only three sides of it are standing and they are riddled with great shell holes.

Six hundred feet beyond this tower were the German trenches. The little island was hardly a hundred feet in its greatest dimension.

I wish I could make those people who think that war is good for a country see that Belgian outpost as I saw it that night under the moonlight. Perhaps we were under suspicion; I do not know. Suddenly the *fusees,* which had ceased for a time, began again, and with their white light added to that of the moon the desolate picture of that tiny island was a picture of the war. There was nothing lacking. There was the beauty of the moonlit waters, there was the tragedy of the destroyed houses and the church, and there was the horror of unburied bodies.

There was heroism, too, of the kind that will make Belgium live in history. For in the top of that church tower for three months a Capuchin monk has held his position alone and unrelieved. He has a telephone, and he gains access to his position in the tower by means of a rope ladder which he draws up after him.

Furious fighting has taken place again and again round the base of the tower. The German shells assail it constantly. But when I left Belgium the Capuchin monk, who has become a soldier, was still on duty; still telephoning the ranges of the gun; still notifying headquarters of German preparations for a charge.

Some day the church tower will fall and he will go with it, or it will be captured; one or the other is inevitable. Perhaps it has already happened; for not long ago I saw in the newspapers that furious fighting was taking place at this very spot.

He came down and I talked to him—a little man, regarding his situation as quite ordinary, and looking quaintly unpriestlike in his uniform of a Belgian officer with its tasseled cap. Some day a great story will be written of these priests of Belgium who have left their churches to fight.

We spoke in whispers. There was after all very little to say. It would have embarrassed him horribly had anyone told him that he was a heroic figure. And the ordinary small talk is not currency in such a situation.

We shook hands and I think I wished him luck. Then he went back again to the long hours and days of waiting.

I passed under his telephone wires. Some day he will

telephone that a charge is coming. He will give all the particulars calmly, concisely. Then the message will break off abruptly. He will have sent his last warning. For that is the way these men at the advance posts die.

As we started again I was no longer frightened. Something of his courage had communicated itself to me, his courage and his philosophy, perhaps his faith.

The priest had become a soldier; but he was still a priest in his heart. For he had buried the German dead in one great grave before the church, and over them had put the cross of his belief.

It was rather absurd on the way back over that path of death to be escorted by a cat. It led the way over the fascines, treading daintily and cautiously. Perhaps one of the destroyed houses at the outpost had been its home, and with a cat's fondness for places it remained there, though everything it knew had gone; though battle and sudden death had usurped the place of its peaceful fireside, though that very fireside was become a heap of stone and plaster, open to winds and rain.

Back to Headquarters

Again and again in destroyed towns I have seen these forlorn cats stalking about, trying vainly to adjust themselves to new conditions, cold and hungry and homeless. We were challenged repeatedly on the way back. Coming from the direction we did we were open to suspicion. It was necessary each time to halt some forty feet from the sentry, who stood with his rifle pointed at us. Then the officer advanced with the word.

Back again, then, along the road, past the youthful sentry, past other sentries, winding through the barbed-wire barricade, and at last, quite whole, to the House of the Barrier again. We had walked three miles in front of the Belgian advanced trenches, in full view of the Germans. There had been no protecting hedge or bank or tree between us and that ominous line across. And nothing whatever had happened.

Captain Fastrez was indignant. The officers in the House of the Barrier held up their hands. For men such a risk was legitimate, necessary. In a woman it was foolhardy.

Nevertheless, now that it was safely over, they were keenly interested and rather amused. But I have learned that the gallant captain and the officer with him had arranged, in case shooting began, to jump into the water, and by splashing about draw the fire in their direction!

We went back to the automobile, a long walk over the shell-eaten roads in the teeth of a biting wind. But a glow of exultation kept me warm. I had been to the front. I had been far beyond the front, indeed, and I had seen such a picture of war and its desolation there in the center of No Man's Land as perhaps no one not connected with an army had seen before; such a picture as would live in my mind forever.

Chapter Five

The conclusion of World War I marked a seismic shift in the social and economic roles of women, as their participation in the workforce expanded dramatically in many parts of the world. The war had demonstrated women's ability to perform jobs traditionally held by men, and this reshaped perceptions of gender roles in the workplace.

After the war, many countries experienced a push to return to the *status quo ante*. In the U.K. and the U.S., men returning from the frontlines were reintegrated into civilian life, which meant reclaiming jobs that women had temporarily occupied. Employers and labor unions pressured women to return to domestic roles, arguing that their wartime work was a temporary necessity rather than a permanent shift. Many women were dismissed or demoted to make way for male workers, and social expectations again favored the ideal of the "homemaker."

However, with millions of dead soldiers and a corresponding number of "surplus women," becoming a homemaker was an aspiration that was out of reach for many women. The war had fundamentally altered the demographic landscape, and this meant that, in certain cases, changes that were wrought by the war could not be undone. While the immediate post-war years saw a decline in female workforce participation in industrial sectors, women in many countries began to pursue work in new sectors, particularly in white-collar jobs. Clerical work, for instance, became a field where women found long-term employment. The growing demand for typists, secretaries, and office managers allowed women to establish a more permanent presence in the labor market. In the U.S., the number of women in the workforce rose by more than 25% between 1920 and 1930, and similar trends were seen in other parts of the world.

The increase in women's workforce participation post-WWI had profound social and economic implications. Financial independence gave women a newfound sense of agency and the ability to express increased independence.

Many women, particularly those in urban areas, began to experience life outside of marriage and domesticity. This was a period of burgeoning freedom in dress, behavior, and lifestyle, exemplified by the "flapper" culture of the 1920s, where young women challenged conventions of modesty and Victorian ideas of decorum.

Economically, the entry of women into the workforce contributed to broader changes in society, including the growth of consumer culture. With disposable income of their own, women became a significant market demographic, influencing everything from fashion to household goods. This, in turn, shaped industries, advertising, and media portrayals of women. The rise of female workers also underscored the need for policy reforms, leading to incremental improvements in labor rights, such as maternity leave and the fight for equal pay, which would gain momentum in the decades to come.

Despite these advancements, women continued to face considerable challenges in the post-WWI era. Wage disparities persisted. This arose due to the fact that, prior to World War I, the assumption of employers was that they had to pay a laborer enough to support an entire family. After World War I, the notion of the family-structure had eroded, with employers relating to their workers as "individuals". (One pays an individual, responsible for only one person, much less than one would pay a breadwinner responsible for supporting an entire family.)

This assertion of the 'individual" as the new basis for society (rather than the family) was a tectonic shift underwritten by the expansion of the vote. Prior to the war, the assumption was that a man was voting to advance the interests of his entire family. With the notion of "one person, one vote," the focus shifted from the family to the individual.

The importance of this change cannot be overstated. Ever since Aristotle in "Politics," the assertion was that the family was the nucleus of the state. He writes, "Since it is now evident of what parts a city is composed, it will be necessary to treat first of family government, for every city is made up of families."

He states that the basic unit is the family. Once you get cousins living around a particular family, you get a tribe. And, once you get a number of tribes, you get a nation. But he stresses over and over again that it is the family that is at the center of a civilization.

After World War I, the idea gained traction that the individual was the basis for the society. As a result, the family was shunted to the side. And one of the unfortunate ramifications of this was the aforementioned tendency of businesses to no longer pay one enough to support a family, but, rather, to support a single individual. With an expansion of the labor pool as women entered the workforce, a downward pressure was placed on wages as more people competed for fewer jobs. This benefited employers, who would offer ever lower wages as they sang the praises of "individualism" to their workers.

In the face of these challenges, women continued to organize and advocate for greater rights and recognition. The interwar years saw a rise in feminist movements which were fueled by millions of surplus women from the war, who sought a place in society and agitated for more political representation. The suffrage movements, which gained traction during the war, achieved major victories in countries like the United States (1920) and the United Kingdom (1918). These gains would be crucial as women continued to push for greater access to the workforce in the decades to follow.

In the 1930s, the economic hardships of the Great Depression further complicated women's efforts to break into industries, as many believed that men should be prioritized for jobs. However, World War II brought another wave of opportunity. Women once again filled critical roles in industries, particularly in the defense sector, as millions of men were drafted into military service. In the U.S., programs like "Rosie the Riveter" became symbols of women's industrial contribution, as they worked in factories, shipyards, and other industrial settings. By the end of the war, nearly six million American women had entered the workforce.

After World War II, the post-war economic boom and the rise of consumerism created new opportunities for women. It wasn't, however, until the 1960s and 1970s that women were permanently integrated into the labor pool as a major factor. This time-period saw women begin to enter managerial and professional roles in larger numbers. Women's participation in business schools and graduate programs also rose during this time, creating a path for them to break into industries such as finance, law, and media.

The 1980s and 1990s marked the rise of a new generation of female leaders in industry, business, and government. With more women earning advanced degrees, they began to make strides in traditionally male-dominated fields such as banking, technology, and corporate management. By 1997, women in the United States accounted for 55 percent of college enrollments, with men down to 45 percent.

At the same time, women's presence in industries such as technology and medicine grew. In the 1980s, female participation in STEM (Science, Technology, Engineering, and Mathematics) fields remained limited, but programs encouraging women and girls to pursue careers in science and technology began to gain momentum. The government began to fund programs for girls and to award grants to females which, as of the 21st Century, are creating a gender imbalance in the workplace that is now favoring women for the first time.

Intellectuals like Christina Hoff Sommers have set up a warning that these policies were so successful that the over-correction may now be disadvantaging males. In her book "The War Against Boys," she argues that this imbalance, driven by well-intentioned efforts to empower girls, has resulted in a system where boys are increasingly neglected.

Sommers' central argument is that many programs and policies designed to promote gender equality for girls have had unintended consequences for boys, particularly in academic settings. She critiques the way society, schools, and the media often portray boys' struggles as a natural or unimportant part of advancing female equality.

She and other likeminded social critics point out that in the United States and many other Western countries, girls consistently graduate high school at higher rates than boys. According to data from the U.S. Department of Education, for every 100 girls who earn a high school diploma, only about 90 boys do so. This trend has contributed to a growing gap in college enrollment and completion rates, with women outpacing men in higher education. As of 2022, about 60% of college students in the U.S. are women, a shift from previous decades when men were the majority.

In academia, the disparity in college enrollment has translated into a higher proportion of women occupying roles as educators, administrators, and students. In some areas, such as elementary and secondary education, women have become the overwhelming majority of employees. This gender shift has created an environment where male educators and students are the minority, which may inadvertently reinforce gender-based biases and assumptions that further marginalize boys.

Sommers also critiques the use of gender-based hiring initiatives and quotas intended to increase female representation in certain industries. While these initiatives have been crucial for rectifying historical imbalances, she argues that in some fields, they have led to discrimination against male candidates. For example, STEM fields have seen a concerted effort to increase female participation, sometimes to the extent that qualified male candidates are overlooked or disadvantaged in favor of meeting gender quotas.

In certain professions, such as nursing and human resources, women not only dominate the workforce but have also become preferred hires for many positions. In some cases, these gender-skewed fields offer better job security and benefits than male-dominated sectors. The shift toward greater female representation in these high-demand fields has left men disproportionately underrepresented, mirroring the historic imbalances that women have fought to overcome in male-dominated sectors like finance and engineering.

Among younger generations of workers, particularly those in urban areas, women are now out-earning men in several professions. A Pew Research study found that in 22 of the largest U.S. cities, young women in their 20s and early 30s earn more than their male counterparts. In ten metropolitan areas in the study, women earned 102% of what men earned.

"As the education gap gets bigger between men and women, the wage gap gets smaller," said Pew Research senior researcher and 2022 study author Richard Fry. "With a decline in manufacturing and other professions men were dominant in and the rise in health and education jobs that women often get, young women have caught up to men in income," Fry said.

As social dynamics change and the nature of the economy evolves, we are seeing (and will *continue* to see) paradigm shifts that change the story of women—a story whose outlines came into focus due in large part to World War One.

Without that catalyzing event, we wouldn't have seen the tremendous social changes wrought by, say, Alva Myrdal (the mother of the Swedish welfare state) in the 1930s. Or Beatrice Potter Webb, her counterpart in the United Kingdom in the 1940s.

We wouldn't have witnessed the rise of female entrepreneurs like Coco Chanel with her eponymous fashion empire, or Sara Blakely the founder of the billion-dollar company Spanx.

In the 21st Century, we've likewise seen the rise of leaders like Sheryl Sandberg (COO of Facebook), Mary Barra (CEO of General Motors), and Ginni Rometty (former CEO of IBM), highlighting the significant strides women have made in the corporate world.

Moreover, women have achieved notable advances in science, like Rosalind Franklin, whose research into X-ray diffraction images was critical to the discovery of DNA. Or Dorothy Hodgkin, who won the Nobel Prize in Chemistry in 1964 for her work determining the structures of important biological molecules, including penicillin, insulin, and vitamin B12. Her research laid the groundwork for modern pharmaceutical developments.

With an increased footprint in academia and the consequent augmentation of economic power comes increased political power.

As the 20th century progressed, women began to rise to positions of global prominence in public affairs. Christine Lagarde, for example, became one of the most powerful women in global finance, first as the Managing Director of the International Monetary Fund (IMF) and later as the President of the European Central Bank. Her leadership in these roles has had a significant impact on global economic policies.

In the decades following World War One, women became heads of state in countries across the world, breaking long-standing gender barriers. Notable examples include Indira

Gandhi in India, Margaret Thatcher in the United Kingdom, Angela Merkel in Germany, Jacinda Ardern in New Zealand, and so forth. None of this would have been possible before World War One.

And as larger sociological changes get under pace, this trend will not slacken, but pick up.

In a 1974 book entitled "A Time to Choose: America's Energy Future," McGeorge Bundy outlines how the United States, to counteract the energy crisis, will transition from an industrial economy to a post-industrial economy. He correctly predicted that, as the America of the 21st Century shifts away from industry, factory jobs would be less common. Instead, he said, the U.S. would see an increase in sectors like government, education, healthcare, and insurance. The latter are fields that heavily favor women.

For much of the 19th and 20th centuries, industrial jobs such as manufacturing, mining, and construction were the backbone of Western economies. These fields were dominated by men, not only due to the physical nature of the work but also because of the cultural expectations and gender roles of the time. However, with globalization, automation, and technological advancements, many industrial jobs have disappeared or relocated to other parts of the world where labor is cheaper. According to the U.S. Bureau of Labor Statistics, between 2000 and 2020, the U.S. manufacturing sector shed nearly 5 million jobs.

In contrast, the sectors that are expanding—healthcare, education, and business services—are traditionally dominated by women. According to the World Economic Forum, over 75% of healthcare workers in OECD countries are women, and women make up the majority of educators in early and primary education. These sectors are not only growing but are also becoming more critical as societies age and demand for healthcare and education rises.

The knowledge economy—focused on information, services, and innovation—also aligns well with skills where women tend to excel. Research shows that women are often better represented in fields requiring communication, collaboration, and emotional intelligence, which are becoming increasingly valued in business and leadership roles. As automation replaces routine tasks, jobs that require these "soft skills" are less likely to be automated, further entrenching women's foothold in these growing industries.

The upshot is that we're living in a society now where unprecedented opportunities are open to women, which translates into political power.

While the Story of Women is not done being written, it is no understatement to say that a major plot-twist occurred in the years between 1914 and 1918, when World War One happened—a paradigm shift whose consequences will radiate out for centuries to come.